"Zig Ziglar's optimism will be a legacy that will forever impact our history."

—Paul Harvey, Paul Harvey News

"When I first heard Zig, my lecture career was limited to drug abuse prevention. My message was angry, punitive and unforgiving because I had lost a daughter to LSD. Zig's hopeful, loving, and forgiving words quickly persuaded me to change and follow his positive attitude about life's great problems. Thanks, Zig . . . it's been a great twenty-five years!"

—Art Linkletter

"Over the years, I have witnessed Zig's impact on people. Undoubtedly, those who hear him speak make positive changes in their lives as it is impossible to hear him and not be moved."

—Richard DeVos, President, Amway Corporation

"Zig Ziglar epitomizes determination, perseverance, excellence, and a loving Christian spirit more than anyone I know! The world would be a better place if more of us were just like him."

—Kenneth H. Cooper, M.D.,
The Cooper Clinic, Dallas, Texas

"Zig Ziglar inspires his listeners to reach for their highest and enjoy life to the fullest . . . He has made the world a better place, one person at a time."

—Mike Huckabee, Governor of Arkansas

"No man in the whole business world has ever impacted the lives of so many for good as has Zig Ziglar. His presence with the people of God has been a benediction to untold thousands. It is my humble prayer that the Lord in heaven will continue to sanctify his every word and his every effort to bring the Good News of what is best for us to all who will hear him."

—W. A. Criswell, Pastor Emeritus,
First Baptist Church, Dallas, Texas

Juanell Teague is a business coach and founder of People Plus, Inc., a Dallas-based consulting company to businesses and individuals seeking to develop or enhance careers as professional speakers. Juanell, who has worked with celebrity speakers such as Zig Ziglar, Dr. Norman Vincent Peale, and Art Linkletter, lives in the Dallas area. **Mike Yorkey** is the author, coauthor, or general editor of fifteen books, including *Touched by the Savior* and *Daddy's Home*. He was the editor of *Focus on the Family* magazine for eleven years, and currently lives in the San Diego area with his family.

THE ZIG ZIGLAR DIFFERENCE:

How the Greatest Motivational Speaker of the Century Has Changed Lives—And How He Can Change Yours

Juanell Teague with Mike Yorkey

Berkley Books, New York

THE ZIG ZIGLAR DIFFERENCE

This book is an original publication of The Berkley Publishing Group.

A Berkley Book / published by arrangement with
the author

PRINTING HISTORY
Berkley trade paperback edition / August 1999

The Penguin Putnam Inc. World Wide Web site address is
http://www.penguinputnam.com

ISBN: 0-425-16873-5

BERKLEY®
Berkley Books are published by The Berkley Publishing Group,
a division of Penguin Putnam Inc.,
375 Hudson Street, New York, New York 10014.
BERKLEY and the "B" design
are trademarks belonging to Penguin Putnam Inc.

PRINTED IN THE UNITED STATES OF AMERICA

10 9 8 7 6 5 4 3 2 1

To my mother and role model, Mamie Wood, who gave me the greatest gift of all—the gift of meaningful values. It was with that gift that I was able to take Zig Ziglar's philosophy and make it work for me.

And to Paul Sides, whose financial assistance gave birth to this project and helped both of our dreams come true.

Acknowledgments

With a book of this magnitude, there are many people to thank for their assistance in helping to see it to fruition.

First and foremost, this acknowledgment goes to my husband, James, who was responsible for teaching me to follow the nudge of the Holy Spirit.

I also want to acknowledge my Wednesday night Bible study group: Guy and Bobbie Andrews; Harry and Mae Green; Steve and Lynn Heffner; Ken and Margie Perry; and Lathan and Barbara Garnett. Their unconditional love has meant a lot to me. Next is the Highland Oaks Church of Christ, where James and I have worshipped since we moved to Dallas more than a decade ago.

The entire Zig Ziglar project would not have happened without Laurie Magers and Elly Mixsell. God gave me His top angels when He sent Laurie and Elly to work with me. Another person who has been very supportive has been Nancy Riddick, my personal assistant, who puts magic into the letters coming out of my office.

Richard Moore, who is the best copywriter in Dallas, helped me write the original book proposal. His input was invaluable.

Marsha McClelland, who conducted the interviews for this book, was an incredible help. Kathy McInnis, who transcribed those interviews, continually insisted, "Juanell, you cannot quit. These stories must get out."

Dr. Janet Novotny deserves my thanks for her ability to help me communicate more clearly in writing my final thoughts in the book.

The MasterMind Group provided unfailing emotional support. Bryan Flanagan, Vickie Henry, James Huggins, James Parker, Bob Rausch and Al Fike were wonderful.

Paul Chantilis, who volunteered to organize the Zig Ziglar Tribute dinner, has been there every step of the way, as has Del Rogers with his guidance on fund-raising for the event.

Another special acknowledgment goes to Bob Lightner, whose support has been tremendous, and to Terry Parker, who helped me set up the not-for-profit Ziglar Tribute organization. John Jenkins's willingness to take on more every day with the tribute dinner was unbelievable to me.

To the Zig Ziglar Tribute board of directors—Lou Holtz, Dave Hurley, Bernie Lofchick, Peter Lowe, Dr. Frank Minirth, Dennis Parker, Nido Qubein, Jim and Naomi Rhode, D. W. Rutledge, and Mark Warren—thank you for acting as fervent supporters and committed advisors.

I want to acknowledge those individuals who are committed to carrying on our dream: Kep Kepner, Idell Moffett, Harriet Meyerson and Honor Bell. Jim Kirk, one of the most outstanding meeting planners in the country, graciously committed to producing the Ziglar Tribute dinner.

Glen Christopher deserves thanks for helping us with our Web site. Karen Karinja, in charge of the leadership program in the Richardson, Texas, public school district, has been instrumental in getting the word out.

Contents

Foreword xi

Introduction xv

1. Juanell Teague: My Story 1

2. Jan McBarron: Listening to the Inner Voice 11

3. Dave Hurley: From Rags to Reality 21

4. Lou Holtz: Winning One for the Gipper 30

5. Janelle Hail: She Battled Back 35

6. Ed Hearn: A Major League Test 46

7. Linda Warner: Back from the Brink 55

8. Clint Lewis: He Lost His Sight—But Found
His Vision 64

9. Kim Whitham: Guilt That Washed Away 74

10. Trent Gaites: In the Futures Market 85

11. Pam Lontos: Don't Tell Her It's Impossible Until After She's Done It. 94

12. Carolyn Ward: A Mary Kay–Meets–Zig Ziglar Success Story. 103

13. Christopher Doyle: The Karate Kid 112

14. Gina Lopez: The Prodigal Daughter 120

15. Chris Leto: Looking Up All the Way. 128

16. Teresa Helgeson: Learning to Prime the Pump . . 138

17. Joe Schoenig: With a Leg to Stand On 148

18. Alexander (Sandy) Berardi: No Longer Under the Curse 154

19. Zig Ziglar: Up Close and Personal. 163

Final Thought 183

Foreword

If you have a vision for it, you can accomplish it. For many years I have had a vision to touch as many lives as possible with a life-changing message and help others to fulfill their own life's missions. I am thrilled to say that over the past decade I have seen that dream fulfilled. However, I could not have seen the tremendous results without the support and encouragement of one very special man—Zig Ziglar.

Zig has been a mentor to me over the last ten years and I have seen firsthand how he has touched the lives of millions of people—equipping them with the power to cultivate the energy of change.

In the volatile business of putting on motivational seminars, a business that I have been so closely associated with over the last few years, there has always been one constant: Zig Ziglar. No other person has so deeply affected the lives of so many people in such a tremendously tangible way. A one- or two-hour session with Zig has motivated the masses for a lifetime.

I am always impressed when I see Zig in action at one of the VIP breakfasts that open all of my SUCCESS Seminars. No matter how many hundreds of people are present to catch a glimpse of their hero, he will never allow anyone to pass without a personal word of greeting.

When starstruck fans shyly sidestep around him, I've seen him sprint over and insist that they introduce themselves to him and share a little of their story. I've also seen the private tears flow down the cheeks of even the most stoic businessmen as they share with Zig the difference that he has made in their families and careers.

The precepts that Zig has so clearly communicated have helped heal marriages, repair broken families, revitalize careers and strengthen work relationships. But more than that, Zig helps people to realize the importance of having an impact on the lives of others. To aspire to personal greatness is noble and good—but to aspire to helping others achieve personal greatness is pure joy.

Like so many people who are featured in this wonderful collection, I have had my share of hardship. I honestly believe that the entire level of your success is defined by your approach to failure.

I look back at my life just a few short years ago and recall the devastating adversity that I had to tackle. I was experiencing a deluge of misfortune, including financial woes, disastrous business situations, critical family health issues and a grueling travel schedule that kept me from my wife and newborn son. This was just the tip of the iceberg in what would turn out to be the most difficult period in my life. I truly felt like Job and was incredibly overwhelmed. It seemed impossible to face all these challenges simultaneously.

Before you start feeling sorry for me, remember that I had an open line with one of the greatest encouragers: Zig Ziglar. Throughout my personal time of crisis, as I listened to Zig backstage and shared some wonderful moments with him together in prayer and conversation, his time-tested golden nuggets of truth took hold of me and helped remind me of what I needed to do to get back on track.

I respect his counsel. I admire his spiritual walk. But most of all, I cherish his friendship.

His brilliant yet homespun wisdom and philosophy on every aspect of life have entertained us and inspired us over the years. His timeless quotations can be heard in the classroom, the pulpit, the board meeting and around the family dinner table.

German philosopher Arthur Schopenauer once said, "It is when he is off guard that a man best reveals his character." Zig Ziglar is incapable of putting on a front. He never challenges you to take on a task that he, himself, would not be willing to conquer.

I have seen him inspire an audience of twenty thousand with his consistent enthusiasm for life when deep down he was devastated by a very personal and tragic loss within his own family. I have never met anyone so true to his ideals.

I am often amused when we are riding together in an elevator and Zig kindly asks the person in front if he or she would please push the button for his floor. Before long, at least one person recognizes that distinctive voice and will ask if he's really Zig. Never one to resist a captive audience, within that short distance between floors, he has a way of affecting people's lives. I have seen him take the same amount of time and attention with the hotel bellman as he does with a former President of the United States. His special gift of encouragement compels you to want to not only live better but *be* better.

Zig is an amazing architect of people. He helps them

build within themselves the foundational qualities that allow them to maximize success in all areas of their lives—helping them to develop the internal desire to do what it takes to be successful. He does this first by equipping them with the skills they need to accomplish this change and then by reinforcing these new habits on a regular basis. In essence, Zig Ziglar has helped build better people. Don't take my word for it. I have hundreds of letters that have come my way from many individuals at my events whose lives have been forever changed as a result of Zig's message.

His devotion to people is tireless. His energy is boundless. His fierce commitment to excellence is endless. His integrity is forthright. That, my friends, is the mark of a very, very special man.

Peter Lowe

Introduction

I'm going to begin this book by making a pretty strong statement: Zig Ziglar is, without question, the most successful, charismatic and influential speaker of our time.

"When Zig Ziglar says God gave him a strong voice, he sells himself short," wrote Mike Steere in *Worth* magazine. "We have here a human cathedral organ. Zig could exhort the crowd to floss regularly and water the houseplants, and 10,000 people would take notes. The rest would be too carried away to write."

Mr. Steere is using hyperbole, of course, but I have found Zig to be a serious thinker on the issues of self-discovery, and a man of self-improvement and enhanced achievement. Nobody in his field has the ability to inspire like Zig.

He's also a best-selling author. For more than twenty-five years, each new Zig Ziglar book has expanded his philosophy and produced another generation of success stories. Presenting his package of super salesmanship, balanced life approach and enhanced powers of persuasion, Zig has a unique vision of integrity, ethics and success in more-than-material terms. His influence is everywhere: A quick survey of the Internet using the key words "Zig Ziglar" produced an astounding 9,346 matches.

At the same time, no book has yet documented the defining moment that made him Zig Ziglar. No book has laid out the ways in which Zig's philosophy has prepared famous and not-famous men and women to seize their defining moments and step into lives that made a difference.

Defining moments. I believe that in every person's lifetime, there comes a defining moment when a decision can set the direction of that person's life for years, if not decades. These all-too-brief moments are sometimes called "windows of opportunity," but I prefer the term "turning points" or "turning point nudges."

Turning point nudges are earmarked by an overpowering feeling of urgency or inspiration to take action. We often discount the nudges we receive because of the risk involved in behaving outside our normal pattern. I've learned that a nudge lasts only a few minutes, but if you act on it, it can tremendously impact your personal and business life.

Similarly, Zig believes that taking control of our future allows us to add immeasurable value to our lives. This empowering act gives us purpose and the confidence to be the best we can be.

That's why the book you're holding will show you how people's lives were changed when they acted upon Zig's life-changing message. As they describe their defining moments, you will be better equipped to recognize and step through your own turning points.

Throughout the many years of my career as a business coach to the speaking industry, I have helped many people from diverse backgrounds—business, industry, entertainment and sports—use professional speaking as a way to affect positive social reform beyond their original areas of interest. I have been privileged in assisting them to find their real meaning and purpose in life—and the desires of their hearts.

Interestingly, a high percentage of these speakers and leaders acknowledged a debt to Zig and his teachings. I, of course, felt the same way. We'd swap stories of Zig-inspired revelation, the wonderful changes he brought to our lives, and discovered we belong to the same fraternity. It was striking how many exceptional human beings marked their transition from ordinary to extraordinary by a moment of Ziglarized self-discovery. It is their stories that have made this book inevitable.

One of my clients, Mary LoVerde, likes to tell this cute anecdote about how much Zig Ziglar has become a part of her life—and her family's.

As a big fan of Zig's, Mary often played his tape series on the family's audiocassette player while caring for her three small children. One day, her five-year-old son Nicholas came home from kindergarten and proudly handed her his paper.

"We studied the letter Z today, and I drew pictures," he announced with pride in his voice.

Mary stooped down and looked at the large piece of construction paper with several primitive drawings. The first picture appeared to be several animals behind a fence.

"Is this a zoo?" she asked.

"Yes, Mommy!"

The next picture looked roughly like a four-legged animal with black-and-white stripes.

"I bet this one is a zebra," said Mary.

Nicholas's face beamed.

The next picture was a stick man. Mary wasn't sure

what to say. "Gee, honey, this is a lovely picture of a man. But 'man' starts with an M, not a Z."

"That's not a man," he retorted. "That's Zig Ziglar!"

Mary laughed. She knew Zig was famous, but famous enough to become a household name in kindergarten?

Why not? Zig Ziglar's message of hope and encouragement resonates with any audience, young or old, down-and-out or well-to-do. Not surprisingly, however, it was Zig himself who brought this project to critical mass. He reveals in his books and his speeches clues to his "before" story that are as gritty, desperate and disappointing as any I've heard. His was a story of deal after deal that crumbled, money that didn't last and happiness that eluded his grasp. For all his brilliance, and until his defining moment, even Zig Ziglar was a failure. He had to step through his turning point nudge to embrace his calling, which was to share his message with the highest degree of burning integrity.

When I proposed this book idea to Zig, I feared that he might find it self-serving, and at first I think he saw this book as a threat to the deep humility that's the core of his being. Only when he was sufficiently reassured that this book was not merely a tribute, but filled with valuable lessons, did he give me his blessing to proceed with the project.

This book will not be simply a long list of people saying, "Zig Ziglar changed my life, and I'm happier and healthier because of it." Zig thought the book could offer significant value only if the people would be specific about the position they were in and the changes they made in their lives. The people you are about to meet in this book are those who had the courage and faith to follow Zig's example and meet him "at the top." Both Zig and I hope you, too, will be able to recognize life's turning points and make the changes necessary to be the best you can be.

Juanell Teague

My Story

Twenty years ago, I was a housewife—a classic Suzy Homemaker. My desire in life was to be best wife, mother and homemaker God ever put on this earth. While I believe I was reasonably successful, I felt unfulfilled. This wasn't because I didn't want to be a housewife; it just wasn't enough.

I will never forget the day I realized this—January 19, 1977. I was sitting in the living room of my modest West Texas home, staring out the window, watching one of the worst dirt storms turn our front yard into a dust bowl. As I watched the wind bending the trees to the breaking point, I felt a kindred spirit with those tall oaks: I, too, was at my breaking point. I felt the need to do something *more* with my life. I was filled with a great desire to accomplish something; only I didn't know what that something was.

My mother, my greatest role model, had given me strong family values while I grew up on our farm in Floyd County, Texas. One of those values was that women should be content being great wives and mothers. The idea of having some sort of career—even if it was something "on the side"—was foreign to the Southern Christian culture in which I was raised. But I began to question those values.

I guess this vague feeling of unrest started to surface a few years earlier. I attempted to quell it by taking a position selling athletic equipment for AMF American in early 1975. With no clear picture of my needs or motivations, however, it wasn't surprising that I experienced little success.

Sitting on that living room couch, I took stock: my formal education had stopped short of college; I got married at seventeen. I had spent my time, energy and effort putting my husband through college and raising our family. At age thirty-five, life was one financial struggle after another as we attempted to get by on my husband's salary from the university. I was successfully raising three boys, which gave me much satisfaction, but I felt inadequate by society's standards, both economically and personally.

On that windswept January morning, I can remember staring at a medical bill for $108 and wondering how I could ever pay it. *God, there has to be more to life than this,* I thought.

Staring at the swirling dust storm, I resolved to never spend another day feeling like that for as long as I lived. I was desperate to find some answers in my search for meaning in life.

Books, I thought. *Books contain answers.*

I got in my car and headed to the South Plains Mall. If anyone saw me leave the neighborhood, they must have thought I was crazy to go out in the blinding dust storm. As the gale-force winds rocked the car and the sand impaired my vision, all I could think about was getting to the mall bookstore.

The sand had already piled up in the entryway of the

deserted mall as I walked through the doors and headed straight for the bookstore. I approached the clerk with my request.

"When I was a little girl," I began, "my mother read me a book. It was called *The Power of Positive Thinking*, and she said it was the best book she ever read. Do you have any books like that?"

"We sure do," she replied. "We've got two shelves back there. That's the self-help section."

"Self-help. That's what I need!"

For the next two hours, I sat and devoured every morsel I could find. There were so many treasures on those shelves; I wanted them all. What I was discovering was a whole new way of thinking. I made a snap decision: I charged $125 worth of books on my credit card. I knew if I invested $125, I would get my money's worth. That was the beginning of a commitment.

Among my new collection were Catherine Ponder's *Prosperity Thinking* and *The TNT Inside of You: You Can Sell Anything* by Frank Ponder and *Think and Grow Rich* by Napoleon Hill. And of course I purchased *The Power of Positive Thinking* by Dr. Norman Vincent Peale, the one cherished by my mother.

I couldn't wait to get home and read each volume from cover to cover. I plopped down on the living room couch and didn't do anything else but read. With each passing chapter, I could see a brighter ray of light at the end of the tunnel. I felt both relieved and uplifted.

As soon as my husband, James, came home, I began talking a mile a minute, giving him all this newfound information as fast as I could.

"Did you know you can control your subconscious mind?" I asked him. I learned that in a book called *Psy-*

chocybernetics by Dr. Maxwell Maltz. I never knew that I could start to control my mind.

All the information I was giving James didn't seem to impact him the way it had impacted me. It didn't matter; I had already decided that it was my personal mission to share my discoveries with all my friends. No one could shut me up!

Through the winter and spring months, I bought more books and started my personal self-help library. One evening in early June, at a church supper, I was again telling everyone within earshot about all the motivational books I was reading. A friend, Dennis Menzer, asked me if I had ever heard of Zig Ziglar.

"No, what's a Zig Ziglar?" I replied. I had never heard his name before.

Dennis said he had listened to Zig Ziglar at a convention for elementary school principals, and afterward, he had purchased his book *See You at the Top.*

That was all the information I needed. On a beautiful summer day, June 10, 1977, *See You at the Top* was in my hands. When I read the book, it seemed to have been written just for me. *I can't believe a man thinks this way,* I thought, because this man was describing me. I had everything that this man talked about, but I had not given it any worth.

See You at the Top was different from the fifty or so other books sitting on my new bookshelf. Zig Ziglar spoke of the same values my mother gave me. There was a down-to-earth quality that I could relate to. He zeroed in on all my self-defeating thoughts and jolted me to realize that I had real value.

Emboldened, I ignited my sales career, and before

long I was dealer of the year for AMF, selling more gymnastic equipment (primarily trampolines) than Oshman's, a national sporting goods chain.

My newfound belief in myself and Zig's message prompted me to want to share it with my hometown of Lubbock, Texas. With a resolve that was still new to me, I picked up the phone and called Mr. Ziglar's office in Dallas and ordered six tickets to hear him speak there. Next, I called five of my friends and invited them to go with me. These friends were handpicked because of their positive and supportive attitudes, and I bought them each a copy of *See You at the Top.* I had to prime the pump, as we say in West Texas.

As I sat in the crowd of Zig Ziglar fans, I didn't realize at the time that I was listening to the most outstanding motivational speaker in the world. That's because I had never heard anyone else speak. When he was done, all I knew was that this was a man whose message had to be heard.

At the end of the seminar, I sent my friends off to the display tables because I didn't want them to know what I was about to do. Having gained the courage I needed from Zig's book, I marched down the aisle in my green polyester pantsuit (this was the seventies, remember) and big floppy sun hat with a ribbon hanging down the back. I was scared to death, but determined as well.

Mr. Ziglar was sitting at a table autographing books. When it was my turn to have my book signed, I took a deep breath and asked him, "Mr. Ziglar, what would it take to get you to come to Lubbock, Texas? I promise you a crowd just like this."

He looked up and smiled. "Well, it will take an invitation," he said, as he pulled a business card from his lapel pocket. He wrote his secretary's name on it—Laurie Magers—and said to call her.

I thanked him profusely, and in my mind, it was a done deal. On the drive home, I told all my friends what I had done. They were incredulous.

When I told my husband what I had done, I was scared of what his response would be. If he did not respond favorably, I would not proceed. Then James surprised me. "If you think you can do it, go for it," he said.

I'll never forget that. He *believed* in me. Heartened, but with no background or qualifications, I threw myself into the task of organizing a motivational rally, even though I had no firm commitment from Mr. Ziglar. I wrote him several times and followed up with phone calls, but I could never receive an up or down response out of his office. All that I was told was that my request was still "under consideration."

I would not be deterred. I booked a 3,000-seat auditorium at Texas State University. I walked on that empty stage and looked at those three thousand empty seats, visualizing them being filled. I then borrowed money from the bank. Actually, I borrowed money from three banks. In 1977, a law had been passed to allow a woman to apply for a signature loan, assuming her husband and marriage had good credit. All this was so new to me that I didn't know where to start, but I had been reading everything, including Mark O. Haroldson's *How to Wake Up the Financial Genius Inside You.* I borrowed $1,000 each from three banks, all due and payable in ninety days.

I forged ahead, planning an event in which the main attraction had not agreed to participate. I sent a telegram to Mr. Ziglar, informing him what I had done. If he didn't respond in forty-eight hours, I was ready to fly to Dallas on Southwest Airlines. If I had to sit in his office for twelve, twenty-four, or thirty-six hours, I would do it. I would not leave until he promised to come.

The trip was never necessary. Within twelve hours of his receiving my telegram, the telephone rang. Laurie Magers was on the line.

"Mr. Ziglar's going to give you that date," she said, and it was like a million light bulbs went off in my head. The excitement tingled.

Then I had a few questions. "Should this be reserved seating or by general admission?" I asked Laurie.

"That decision is the producer's responsibility," she replied smoothly, knowing that I was the producer. "Mr. Ziglar just shows up."

Had she taken her fist and hit me in the stomach as hard as she could, she could not have knocked the wind out of my stomach any more than that statement had. Now I was facing reality. What in the world had I done?

Fear began to set in. And then I remembered. *If there's a book written on it, you can figure it out.*

I rushed back to the mall. A new book had just come out that week: *Publicity: How to Get It.* I read all twenty-one chapters and followed all the advice—except the part about staging a publicity stunt. My goal was to sell three thousand tickets.

On February 28, 1978, I picked up Mr. Ziglar at the Lubbock airport. My passion had swayed him to speak at the event, but my inexperience must have been glaringly obvious to him.

As we drove to the arena, Mr. Ziglar asked, "Mrs. Teague, how's it going?"

I reached in the pocket of my suede coat and pulled

out seven tickets. "Mr. Ziglar, we're seven tickets shy of three thousand," I replied, not sure if this was good or bad.

"Mrs. Teague, you don't know what you've done," he said kindly.

The sell-out crowd that evening carried high expectations, as anticipation and excitement filled the auditorium. When I had started promoting the event, I figured 5 percent of Lubbock knew who Zig Ziglar was. Because I had generated media events and press coverage, the name Ziglar dominated the airwaves on the day of the event.

Perhaps that explains why Zig Ziglar was greeted by a standing ovation when I introduced him. From there, things only got better. People absolutely loved him. They laughed and cried and responded in a way that few Ziglar audiences have over the years. Midway through his presentation, Mr. Ziglar asked the crowd if they would be interested in a return engagement. The response was an enthusiastic yes.

"This lady sitting down here is Mrs. Teague," said Mr. Ziglar, "and I haven't said anything to her about this, but I would like to come back in November." This was the first, only and last time he ever did anything like that.

Although I made every rookie mistake you could make, when all was said and done following that first event, I had an unexpected surprise: I actually made money. That possibility had never crossed my mind; all I had wanted to do was share his message.

Zig, as I now call him, returned to do his sales seminar in November, which was another sold-out success. I then thought Lubbock was ready for an all-out motivational rally, with speakers like Dr. Norman Vincent Peale, Art Linkletter, Cavett Robert, Marvin Phillips and, of course,

Zig Ziglar. A year after the premiere Ziglar event, we filled a 7,000-seat arena.

That 1979 event became the seed of People Plus, Inc., a company that I founded. My desire was to represent great speakers, such as Dr. Peale, Art Linkletter and Dr. Denis Waitley, and bring them to the masses where they could lead and inspire.

For the next nine years, I organized successful rallies in forty-three cities, with two hundred programs that reached more than 200,000 people. Many of those listened to best-selling authors and celebrity speakers for the first time. People Plus gained a national reputation, and I was called a "Cinderella" in magazine articles for being an entrepreneurial woman from Lubbock, Texas, who turned her life around and set out to spread the good news.

The schedule was rigorous, and I had to travel to cities three months in advance to help set up offices, make the event happen and see that everyone got paid. Then I had to do it all again somewhere else.

While my work was incredibly fulfilling, the pendulum in my family life had swung too far. I needed some balance. Sure, James had been working with me at People Plus the last couple of years when we were on the road, but we decided to close it down, leave the rally business and move to Dallas, where I would start a business consulting to those in the speaking industry and to those who were aspiring to become speakers.

I became involved with the local chapter of the National Speakers Association and witnessed many struggling speakers. I knew I could help them package their message and send them on their way.

It was during this work that I formed my turning point theory. As I touched upon in the introduction, turning point nudges are not just random or irrational thoughts. They are God talking and directing you. If you follow these nudges, you automatically go where God is working and can best use you.

My turning point happened on January 19, 1977, and if I hadn't acted on that prompting deep within—to get off that couch and go to the bookstore—my life would be very different today. If I had not been exposed to Zig Ziglar, I never would have followed God's stirring in my heart to bring Zig to Lubbock to speak. If I had not brought Zig to Lubbock, I never would have spent nine years producing motivational rallies. If I had never produced motivational rallies, I never would have gained the credibility to become a consultant to those who, like Zig, want to make a difference in people's lives.

I want to thank you, Zig, for giving me a belief in myself. Please allow this book to be a tribute to you and your life.

Jan McBarron

Listening to the Inner Voice

Jan McBarron left the operating bay at Fitzgerald-Mercy Hospital in Darby, Pennsylvania, and headed straight for the break room.

Her work as a nurse was frustrating, and as she lifted a much-needed cigarette to her lips, a cloud of negative thinking surrounded her. She was up to two packs a day, but that wasn't the only vice in her life. She binged on food and drank way too much alcohol in an attempt to erase her unhappiness. Consequently, her weight had ballooned to two hundred pounds.

Great. I'm as big as a beached whale, thought Jan, who was in her early twenties.

Memories of childhood dreams to become a physician crept into her mind. She always swept them away when she remembered that no one in the McBarron family had ever gone to college, let alone considered graduate school. For a female coming of age in the early 1970s, the appropriate health-care career path was nursing school. So Jan tucked her dreams away and did what was expected of her.

As she entered the world of nursing, Jan rapidly excelled and found herself in nursing management. She even went to night school, where she earned her bachelor of science degree in nursing. But as she moved up the ladder, she moved further and further away from daily contact with patients, becoming responsible for more administrative work.

That's ironic, she thought, as she lit another cigarette. Her so-called success in the nursing world had removed her from the nurse-patient relationship that had drawn her to the medical field in the first place.

Jan was unhappy and needed to make some changes in her life. But what were they and how could she make these changes?

A RAY OF HOPE

One evening, Duke Liberatore, Jan's boyfriend at the time (and who has since become her husband), showed up with a set of Zig Ziglar tapes. She pushed the cassettes aside, but the Ziglar tapes seemed to show up everywhere. She would get in the car and find a tape in the cassette deck. She would come home and hear a tape playing in the living room.

Duke, it turned out, was Zig's biggest cheerleader. "This is good. You need to listen to this," he'd say, as he cued up a tape. But Jan wasn't into all that rah-rah stuff.

Slowly but surely, however, Zig's message of hope began to sink in. What impacted her was the startling revelation according to Zig, that, "If you don't like who you are and where you are, don't worry about it because you're not stuck either with who you are or where you are. You can change. You can be more than you are."

Then she heard Zig talk about having the right mental attitude:

Many people will tell you that attitude is the most important thing in life, and I'm inclined to agree with them. Attitude is the beginning point of growth, the concept that yes, you really can do things with your life. Regardless of your field of endeavor, whether it be athletics, sales, medicine, coaching, management, etc., it all begins with your attitude.

One of the things I hear most often about golfers on the PGA Tour is that those who make it are not that much better than those who fail to make it. There are thousands of golfers who, on a casual weekend, score better than some of the touring pros. But under tournament pressure, they don't see themselves as winners and consequently do not succeed on the links.

One thing everybody in America agrees on is that attitude is the difference-maker in life. Attitude has no regard for race, religion, political affiliation, or profession. I often say it's your attitude, not your aptitude, that's going to determine your altitude. Unfortunately, how to build and maintain that attitude is seldom, if ever, taught in America's school systems, yet experience shows it is the determining factor between the good and the great, between those who barely survive and those who make it big.

So it was time, in Zig's words, to get a "checkup from the neck up." Jan realized she had been putting nothing but negative junk into her mind, which made her miserable. Why not try what Zig said? At that moment Jan thought, *I can become a physician.*

But where would she begin? The biggest obstacle, to say the least, would be getting into medical school. The transition from nurse to doctor was simply not accepted, as evidenced by the fact that a bachelor's degree in nursing was not even recognized as a degree that would allow admission into medical school.

As Jan researched her options, she learned that she would have to go back to college and earn a bachelor's degree in biology. Then, if she was admitted to a medical school, she would have to attend for four years, followed by a two-year internship. It would be like climbing Mt. Everest backwards.

However, none of those obstacles deterred her. She would be captain of her ship, not a victim tossed around in the sea of life. She would beat the odds and dare to do what others would not.

FILLED WITH NEGATIVE THOUGHTS

Shortly after Jan began listening to the tapes, she saw several homeless people going through trash cans, digging through garbage for anything they could eat. "Before, I would think, *What dirtballs. What wastes. Why don't you get a job?*" said Jan.

She didn't know it at the time, but all the negative self-talk robbed her of personal energy—the very energy she needed to make changes in her life.

But now, after listening to Zig Ziglar, Jan realized the error of her ways and thought, *Okay, Jan. You've got to say something good. You've got to say something good about them.*

"I thought about it for a little longer, and then I said to myself, *Well, at least they're robbing a trash can and not a bank.* And that was how I found good in homeless people. Not much, but it was a start."

How did Jan use this experience to change her attitude about herself?

"Well, whenever something happened to me, the first thing out of my mouth was negative. I was always complaining about my lot in life or what I saw—like street people rummaging through trash cans. I was a negative person through and through. For years, my mind had been filled with phrases such as, *You're a failure. You're no good. You blew it again. You just binged again. You didn't do your exercise like you thought you would. You didn't say your prayers like you know you should.*

"But after that incident with the homeless, I began thinking two or three positive things to myself, and it all started with the inner voice I learned from the Ziglar tapes. Zig told me that I was not an average person. Those who think they are average will stay that way. 'As a man thinketh, so is he,' said Zig, quoting Proverbs. By taking the steps that Zig said I needed to take, I could take charge of my life and my destiny."

To help feed her mind with positive thoughts, Jan made index cards of affirmation, which she referred to often. This helped her to "lighten up," as she calls it. Then she began to steer away from friends and family members who were too negative. It wasn't that she shunned anybody, but she didn't want to spend much time with folks who told her that she could never become a doctor or that she was a "Benedict Arnold" for leaving the nursing field.

"I found myself gravitating toward people who would give me support and keep me focused," said Jan. "I learned that on the tapes."

RELATIONSHIPS WITH OTHERS

As she began spending more time with positive people, her self-image changed. She started to believe in herself and in others. She stopped blaming the world for everything that wasn't right and started to assume responsibility for herself.

Although Jan knew there would be roadblocks and potholes, she also knew that the destination made it worth the effort of forging ahead. The bottom line was that she felt better. She was happy. What helped her to stay focused was having an emotional, physical, spiritual, career and financial daily action plan.

She wrote her plan down, then listed the obstacles. She named the people who could help her achieve her goals. She set deadlines. On her index cards, she strategized how she could get to where she wanted to be. In working through this process, Jan learned that it would take fifteen years to get where she wanted to be. *That's a long time,* she thought.

So as not to feel completely overwhelmed, Jan set tiny, simple goals. In tackling her health and weight problems, her goals started with these statements: "Today, I'm going to walk for five minutes" or "Today I'm going to drink two glasses of water." She carried her action plan with her and read it every day.

There were times when she cried—often an expression of her anger. So one of her written goals became "Today, I'm going to go through the day and consciously work on smiling more." Another one was "I have a choice to either get upset about something or not get upset about it."

Another thing Jan began doing was singing in the shower each morning. She heard Zig say, "Neither the tune nor your talent for singing is important. The *idea* is the thing. You can't be negative at the top of your voice. As Williams James once said, 'We do not sing because we are happy. We are happy because we sing.' "

One of Jan's major goals was to go back to college and get that degree in biology. She did that. Then it was to be accepted into a medical school. She did that. Then it was to successfully complete four years of medical training. She did that. And finally, she had to complete her two-year residency. Mission accomplished.

Jan became Jan McBarron, M.D., a tremendous accomplishment. But her life changed in other ways, as well. She stopped smoking and quit drinking caffeine and alcohol. She began running regularly, losing enough weight to become a size 7.

So what kind of medicine is Dr. McBarron practicing today? The answer makes sense: bariatrics, the treatment of obesity. Jan has become the fourth female in this country to receive the distinction of being board-certified in the field of bariatrics all the while running two offices, in Columbus, Georgia, and Auburn, Alabama.

Not only does Jan help patients with weight problems, she also treats any medical condition associated with obesity, such as diabetes, high blood pressure, heart disease, arthritis or high cholesterol.

Jan's special touch with patients has attracted media attention. She was asked to host her own television show in Columbus and a nationally syndicated radio show, and she has been a guest on numerous television and radio shows talking about her book *The Columbus Nutrition Program.* That effort, which has sold nearly 900,000 copies, was honored as the only weight-loss book ever to receive the

Reader's Digest Seal of Approval. Her second best-seller is a cookbook called *Flavor Without Fat*.

LIFE TODAY

These days, Jan wears a solid gold turtle necklace, a gift from her husband, Duke, as a symbol that the slow and steady win the race.

In her medical offices, Dr. McBarron encourages her patients to have that same spirit of hope and perseverance. "I always say to my patients, if you had to walk from here to Atlanta, which is 120 miles, you'd feel like you could never do it. But if I asked you to break it down and walk a mile each day for the next 120 days, you would get there."

Another area of enrichment has been her spiritual journey. While she acknowledges that spirituality is a personal thing, Jan learned to set spiritual goals. For her it was to have the Lord more in her life and to not be so judgmental toward the church. The result has been that she feels a greater presence and a greater satisfaction in her life, which had been missing for many years.

WORKING SMART

Jan will be the first to tell you that undergoing a significant personality change and finding career success involves a great deal of effort. "I used to get a little bit miffed when people would say if you just work hard, you can get anything you want," she said. "Actually, working smart is the key. You have to evaluate your work to ensure that your efforts are yielding something and you are not just spinning your wheels. Working hard does not mean working twelve-hour days. I find it's best to work as hard as I can for eight hours and then have the rest of the time to do things I want to do to keep me happy, healthy and balanced.

"The biggest change in my view toward work came after hearing on the Ziglar tapes that working hard is not defined by increased hours, but rather by a good balance. If I could allow myself the luxury of time to relax, I could recharge my batteries and then work better. It was vital to incorporate family, exercise and play into my life. That was a big ah-ha for me."

Keeping a balance isn't easy. One of the most difficult lessons for Jan was learning that sometimes balance is achieved by saying 'no' to certain things that were not consistent with her goals. "This did not come naturally for me. One thing I think women are very guilty of is that we tend to feel like we have this bright red S on our chests—for Superwoman—and we have to be able to do anything. We say yes to everybody and everything. We are nurturing-type individuals, and we tie our self-worth into people's approval of us. If we say no to somebody, they won't approve of us. Therefore, we're going to say yes.

"We can't say yes to everybody and everything. We take on more than we can or should. We bite off more than we can chew, and I think that's when a lot of women end up feeling like failures. I think that was a very important lesson for me. I mean, I'm comfortable now in saying no. If something isn't consistent with my goals, I'm going to say no, and that doesn't make me less of a person."

MORE THAN CONTENTMENT

Contentment was a mere concept that eluded Jan for the first two decades of her life. But as she continues on the journey that began with the introduction of the Ziglar philosophy into her life, Jan is more than content.

The Ziglar message contends that once an individual undergoes the changes that Jan made—acquiring a positive self-image, creating healthy relationships with others and implementing specific goals—then he or she can achieve success for the future. This success is defined in one's health, happiness, relationships, opportunity and overall feeling of well-being. Jan feels a strong sense of peace in her life.

"If I found out that six months from now God was going to say, 'It's over; your time is up,' I wouldn't do anything different that I'm doing right now," she said. "And there are not many people who can say that. I'm very content, but not lazy or complacent.

"The greatest change that Zig brought into my life was not my medical degree. It certainly wasn't losing weight. It's my peace of mind, and anybody can have that. The principles that Zig espouses can certainly make you a better housewife, a better schoolteacher, a better truck driver or a better lineman on an assembly. But my happiness is a decision, and I decided to make that choice."

Dave Hurley

From Rags to Reality

By his own admission, Dave Hurley was "the biggest problem child that ever walked the face of the earth," and you can believe him on this score.

If he wasn't acting up in class, he was pushing kids during recess. After he was arrested for shoplifting, his parents moved him and his five brothers and sisters to Lick Creek, Illinois, a rural burg far from the glittery lights of Chicago.

His parents hoped the change of scenery would do the boy good, but it didn't. It certainly didn't help that Dave was growing up in an oppressive home where no one was allowed to leave the house after school—not for a date, not even for church.

When he was a high school senior, Dave decided *anything* would be better than living in that home, so he ran away and joined the U.S. Marines. You had to be pretty determined to enlist in 1968, during the height of the Vietnam War.

It didn't take long for the drill instructor to figure out this hayseed from southern Illinois.

"Hurley, get in here and get front and center right

now!'' barked the sergeant. The buck private scurried, righted himself and saluted the DI. ''Hurley, you're messing up this entire platoon. On your PT test, the most pull-ups you did was three. The most sit-ups you did were twenty. But you know what bothers me most about you, Hurley? It's your @#$%& attitude!'' screamed the DI at the top of his lungs.

The sergeant wasn't finished with the young recruit. ''Hurley,'' he said, ''you're gonna die in 'Nam. You haven't got a prayer. It's all because you've got a stinkin' attitude.''

''Sir, yes, sir,'' Dave replied.

''Don't 'sir' me,'' spat the DI. ''I don't even want your presence around me. Get out of my sight.''

CHASING THE ALMIGHTY DOLLAR

Dave was shipped out to Southeast Asia, but he managed to survive the war, following a harrowing escape from the Viet Cong. After an honorable discharge, his homecoming was far from triumphant. In those days, Vietnam vets were shunned by much of society, and no one held a welcome-home parade for him.

But life went on, and Dave found a bride, Darlene, and upon their marriage, they moved into a three-room shack that lacked running water. The only electricity was courtesy of an extension cord from a nearby farm.

Dave took a menial job breaking up rocks at an Illinois quarry, but the meager pay barely kept food on the table. ''We were the epitome of poor,'' he said.

One day, a white Cadillac Fleetwood pulled up in his dirt driveway. The man who stepped out was a salesman for waterless cookware—perfect for a newlywed couple without running water.

The salesman was good, and he convinced the young couple that this was something they needed. The Hurleys scraped together the $38.95 down payment and pledged to pay $15 a month until the $400 transaction was completely paid for. But what really got Hurley's attention was the Cadillac, not the cookware.

You see, in the Hurley family, a Cadillac symbolized success, and if the salesman could afford a big Caddy by selling waterless cookware, then Dave wanted to sell waterless cookware.

Dave asked the salesman for a job, but he was turned down flat. Twelve phone calls later, he persuaded the man to give him a shot. Dave took a desperate measure, pawning the only two things of any value that he owned—his guitar and camera—in order to come up with $300 to buy his samples. The pawn was good for ten days.

On Saturday morning, Dave showed up at the salesman's doorstep to collect his cookware. Surprised to see that this young upstart had come up with the $300, the cookware salesman led Dave to the garage, where he handed him a repossessed set of cookware, all scratched and burned.

Dave's new boss wrapped the samples up in newspapers and threw them in an old suitcase. He stuffed in a few order forms that the humidity had melded together, then informed Dave he would be back the following week to train him. Dave didn't have a week. His two prized possessions, his guitar and camera, were at stake.

With no training and no reason to be successful, Dave hit the streets, knocking on doors and telling people, "I'm your everyday street-walkin', door-bangin' salesman. But I've got a neat set of pots and pans. I'd sure like to show them to you."

Dave didn't know that the national average was three sales a week. He made eleven sales that first week. After seeing his initial success, Dave's boss canceled the training session and sent him on his way.

Dave couldn't keep up the sales pace, however, and he soon experienced every kind of problem imaginable. He began failing miserably, and after struggling for a year, he wondered if he had made a huge mistake. Then he heard that a guy named Zig Ziglar, who had also sold cookware, would be speaking at the Checkerdome in St. Louis. *I don't have anything to lose,* thought Dave. *Let's check him out.*

WHAT'S REALLY IMPORTANT

When Dave rolled into the Gateway City, he expected to hear Zig give a point-by-point seminar on how to close a sale.

To his surprise, the seminar was on attitude. "People never care how much we know until they know how much we care—about them," said Zig.

Zig began talking about parables, pointing out that a carpenter from Galilee more than two thousand years ago used parables to teach principles. Far more recently, Zig added, the Center for Creative Research in Greensboro, North Carolina, discovered that using parables was the most effective way of teaching values. "But we also can teach some other significant lessons in life through the use of parables," said Zig, who began to tell one:

> *The story goes that high in the Smoky Mountains a number of years ago, there lived an old man who was a recluse. Though not completely antisocial, he was left pretty much to himself. Somehow, word leaked out that the*

old man was wise in far more things than just what you get out of a book or formal education. It was rumored that he could answer virtually any question anyone might have. With this in mind, a couple of young lads decided to test the old man.

They set a trap and captured a little bird, then made the laborious climb to the mountaintop. They approached the old man with a simple question. One of them said, "Sir, I have a little bird in my hand. My question is: Is the bird dead or alive?"

The old man smiled and wearily said, "That's entirely up to you, son. Whatever my answer is, you have the control. If I say the bird is alive, you could crush the life out of him immediately. If I answer he is dead, you need only open your hands and he will fly away. You see, son, you have the power of life and death in your hands."

Then Zig remarked that in our hands, and more importantly, in our hearts and in our heads, we have the power to be successful or we have the power to fail. "Greatness exists within us," said Zig, "but we must use the ability and intelligence that is inside of us in order to be successful. We just need to remember that if man can take molded bread and produce penicillin, just think what an awesome God can make out of you."

Another Zig story that Dave was particularly drawn to was the one about flea training. A flea can jump thousands of times its height. If confined in a jar, however, the flea will jump up and hit its head on the lid. Eventually, after the flea has repeated this enough times, the lid can be removed and the flea won't jump out of the jar. The reason is simple. The flea has conditioned itself to jump just so high. Once it's done that, that's all it can do.

I've been putting a ceiling on myself, thought Dave. At one time he had dreams and ambitions with no limit, but along the roadway of life, he had bumped his head too many times on the ceiling. He had stopped jumping.

Dave threw himself back into his cookware sales, which improved measurably, but then his world was rocked with the loss of premature twins shortly after their birth. Dave could not shake the depression, and it reflected in his work. Twenty-two days passed without a single sale.

To say money was tight would have been an understatement. On the twenty-second day, without a penny in his pocket, he vowed to his wife that if he didn't make a sale that night, he would go back to work at the rock quarry.

One minor detail: He had no gas to get into town. So Dave rode his bicycle down the Lick Creek blacktop, picking up pop bottles, which he redeemed for two cents apiece. He exchanged them at the local garage for two gallons of gas, which would get his Pontiac Catalina the ten miles to Ana, Illinois, and back.

Knowing that his future hinged on the success of that evening, Dave worked harder that night than he had ever worked in his life. But hours passed without a sale, and at 8 P.M., he walked down Cherry Street toward his car. His future looked bleak.

He passed a man on a ladder, painting the eaves of his house. Dave decided to give it one last shot. "Excuse me, sir," he said as he approached the man. "I'm your everyday street-walkin', door-bangin' salesman. But I've got the neatest set of pots and pans you've ever seen. Can I come in and show them to you, please?"

The man looked down from the ladder and said, "No,

son. We don't need any pots and pans. Thank you, anyhow."

Dave slumped and turned away. He had taken no more than five steps when he heard a voice behind him, "By the way, son, what's bothering you?"

Dave faced the man. "Nothing, sir," he lied. "Everything's fine."

But as he turned toward the street once again, Dave asked himself, *How in the world did this man know? I've never seen him before. How did he know that I am at the very bottom of my life at this moment?*

In an instant, all the words of Zig Ziglar came flooding back into Dave's mind. He turned around, took five giant steps forward, and with a boldness and confidence he'd never imagined he possessed, Dave announced, "Excuse me, sir. I might be your everyday street-walkin', door-bangin' salesman, but I've got the neatest set of pots and pans you've ever seen, and you need to come down off that ladder right now and look at them!"

Charlie Borland looked Dave dead in the eye and said, "That's more like it, son. Let's go take a look." That night, Charlie and his wife, Peggy, bought a set of cookware, and set Dave on a life-changing course.

That cookware purchase reminded Dave that attitude was everything. "I made the decision that day that I would never ever let my attitude control me, and in the future, I would stay in control of my attitude."

To stay in control, Dave began writing down his goals. "A goal gave me a vision, someplace to go," he said. If Dave wrote down, "I'm going to make ten sales next week," he started planning Sunday night. To make ten sales, he calculated that he needed to make two sales a day. He knew from experience that if he made five presentations, he would make two sales. But in order to get one person to look at his cookware, he had to knock on ten doors. So in order to show five people a day, he had to knock on fifty doors. And so the week would begin. And it would inevitably end with a goal met.

WHAT'S IMPORTANT IN LIFE

Flash forward twenty-five years, and today, Dave is owner of Lustre Craft International, the largest distributor of Westbend Waterless Cookware and Kitchen Appliances in the world, doing several million dollars a year in sales.

At first glance, most people would describe this transformation of David Hurley as "rags to riches." That expression, however, is not even a part of his vocabulary. He prefers the phrase "rags to reality" because, in his words, "Reality is to realize that riches are the single least important thing in your life."

What's far more important is attitude. In the world of cookware, Dave's organization is known as "The Positive Company." It all starts when someone is hired at Lustre Craft. He or she is issued Zig Ziglar's complete cassette series, *Secrets of Closing the Sale,* which is followed by other Ziglar tapes as employees move into management.

"I have become a fanatic about it now," Dave admits. "I mean, people come up to me and they know better than to say something negative. They know I will rip it apart and make it into a positive."

For example, if someone asks him how old he is, he replies, "Today? Six hours. I'm six hours old. And tomorrow at 6 A.M. when I get up, I'll be one minute old. Every day to me is a whole brand-new life." Dave reminds himself every morning to smile as he reads a sticker on his mirror that says: "So Much in Life to Enjoy."

That philosophy is heard often at Lustre Craft, where Dave has essentially become the on-staff Zig Ziglar. He started a summer work program specifically for college students, hiring anywhere from six hundred to one thousand students. The training gives the students so much confidence that "if we'd have sent them fishing for Moby Dick, they would have taken tartar sauce," says Dave, stealing a line from his old mentor.

When the students return to their marketing classes in the fall, the professors are astounded at their knowledge of sales, marketing and relating to people. These achievements were recognized by the National Teaching Association and the American Marketing Association, who awarded the program with honors and asked Dave to speak about what brought the drastic changes in the students' lives.

A CHANCE MEETING

For all this emotional attachment to Zig Ziglar, Dave had never met the man until three years ago at a Westbend International convention. Although he had had several opportunities to do it, Dave had never got up the courage to approach his hero.

But this Westbend convention was going to be different. When the moment arrived, Dave pushed his nerves aside and shared with Zig how his message of hope had redefined his life and given him the tools and inspiration to move forward with confidence. Then Dave related how he had carried his message to many in his company. Since that time, Dave and Zig have formed a friendship that, in Dave's words, "is a bond that will be eternal."

Lou Holtz

Winning one for the Gipper

When Notre Dame football fans gather in sports bars and begin friendly arguments about the greatest coaches in Fighting Irish history, you can bet a green beer that Lou Holtz's name is mentioned in the same breath with coaching legends Knute Rockne, Frank Leahy and Ara Parseghian.

Lou Holtz accomplished much while he prowled the sidelines of Notre Dame Stadium. Over an eleven-year span, his Notre Dame teams rang up ten or more victories in seven seasons and won one hundred games, more than any other coach except for the great Rockne. In 1988, with Lou at the helm, the Fighting Irish stiff-armed the competition and won the national championship as the number one team in the country.

More importantly, a Lou Holtz team was always feared, earning a reputation for its ability to knock off highly ranked opponents. One thing you knew with Lou stalking the sidelines with headset and clipboard: The Fighting Irish would always fight until the clock ran out.

But few people know that in the mid-1970s, Lou was at the lowest point in his twenty-seven-year coaching career.

At that time, he was head coach of the New York Jets, a thirty-nine-year-old wunderkind with a reputation for turning around football programs faster than you can say *hut-hut*.

This was the big time. Lou wasn't coaching at William and Mary or North Carolina State, his previous rungs on the coaching ladder. This was New York City, where NFL football was life and death. The glare of the media spotlight in the Big Apple served to magnify the pressure tenfold. With his every coaching move scrutinized and dissected by the media, it wasn't long before Lou was swept up in one coaching controversy after another.

For instance, should Lou play quarterback Joe Namath, the over-the-hill Super Bowl III hero whose arthritic knees limited his mobility, or Richard Todd, the heir apparent from Namath's alma mater, the University of Alabama? What were the Jets going to do about losing running back John Riggins to free agency and the Washington Redskins?

The Jets, who had floundered for several seasons before Lou's arrival, were put on a rebuilding program by Lou. Still, victories were scarce: As his first pro season neared the end, the Jets had won only three of thirteen games.

In the season's final week, Lou and his wife, Beth, talked about their situation. They agreed that they didn't feel comfortable in the big-city environment. They agreed their four children—all under the age of thirteen—were not thriving. They agreed that maybe this NFL coaching position was not for them.

Emboldened, Lou resigned from the Jets just before the final game of the 1976 season. "God did not put Lou Holtz on this earth to coach pro football," he said in a press conference announcing his resignation. "This decision has cost me a lot of agony, but I am at peace with myself." Lou added that he missed the teaching aspect of college football in which he developed a closeness with the players while guiding and building their futures.

A *New York Times* story said, "According to Holtz, he hadn't been himself for quite some time. He hadn't been the same happy-go-lucky guy, the smiler, the chatter. Above all, he hadn't been a college coach." So Lou left New York for the greener pastures of Fayetteville, Arkansas, home of the University of Arkansas Razorbacks.

The first order of business for Lou and Beth was to find a house. They purchased the home of Gene and Jean Hudson.

"We called them 'He Gene' and 'She Jean,' " said Lou. "That home turned out to be one of the greatest homes we've ever had, and we became close friends with the Hudsons."

Gene worked for a supermarket chain called the Mad Butcher, and Zig Ziglar had made a series of speeches before the employees. Gene, sensing a need, handed Lou a set of the Ziglar tapes and encouraged him to give them a listen.

"When I left the New York Jets and came to the University of Arkansas, there were a lot of negative consequences associated with that decision," said Lou. "Even though I was forgetting about the past and was upbeat about my future, my self-esteem was down. I needed to focus on where I was going and what I would be doing."

Lou landed in Fayetteville in early December—prime recruiting season for college football. His normal routine was to hop in the car and begin tooling around the state of Arkansas visiting recruits.

"When you're driving through some sections of the

Ozarks, you don't get many radio stations," said Lou. "It was either listen to nothing or listen to Zig Ziglar, so I chose the latter. Once I put a tape in and started listening, I found his message to be very, very good. He was funny. He was entertaining. The next thing I knew, the tape would be finished, and I would be reaching for the next one. He was that good."

After an hour with Zig, Lou was ready to storm a tackling dummy. His attitude brightened. He felt good about life. Things were going to get better. "Zig has a way of telling stories that you can identify with," said Lou. "There's something in his timing and wording."

Things did get better in a hurry for Lou. Although he was replacing a legendary coach at Arkansas, Frank Broyles, Lou burst onto the scene by guiding the Razorbacks to an 11–1 record and a New Year's Day date at the Orange Bowl against top-ranked Oklahoma.

Between the end of the season and the Orange Bowl, however, Lou made the difficult decision to suspend three of his top players—who had scored 78 percent of the team's touchdowns—for rules infractions. Lou was embroiled in another coaching controversy. A lawyer contacted the three athletes and said he could get a judge to reinstate them for the Orange Bowl. A court date was set.

Lou refused to hire an attorney, but since he was coaching at a state university, he was considered a state employee, so the Arkansas attorney general said he would represent Lou. The attorney general's name was Bill Clinton.

"He did a wonderful job," said Lou, who won the court battle.

Arkansas was a 24-point underdog against Oklahoma, who would be named national champions if they defeated the Razorbacks. But someone forgot to tell Lou and his young charges, who stormed the field and manhandled second-ranked Oklahoma, 31–6, even without the three star players. It was one of the great upsets in college football history.

"That first year in Arkansas was a traumatic experience, moving the family twice in twelve months, being in a new state, not knowing anybody," said Lou. "When I came across Zig Ziglar's tapes, they were a godsend. He told stories I could identify with and helped me gain a mental edge. I know his religious beliefs and philosophy strengthened my faith. I became a big fan of his."

When his children became teenagers and they asked Lou for something significant—a new bike, going to summer camp—Lou would say, "If you will read *See You at the Top* and discuss it with me intelligently, your chances will be greatly enhanced that I will say yes."

So Lou's children became Ziglarized.

When Lou moved on to Notre Dame, he took Zig with him. By this time, he and Zig had struck up a friendship, and Lou would call Zig as a sounding board. One year, before a big bowl game, Lou asked Zig to talk to the Fighting Irish football players, to buck them up before the big game.

"I've met a lot of people in my day, and what I found out about Zig after knowing him is that everything he writes and says he lives by," says Lou. "That has not always been the case with people I've known, but Zig is different. I can't say enough things about him as a friend, as an individual and as a leader."

Janelle Hail

She Battled Back

For Janelle Hail, life in the late 1970s was as picture perfect as the family photos she hung with care in the hallway of her stylish home. She was a young mother of three boys. Beautiful family. Nice neighborhood. Caring friends.

Yet lurking beneath this happy exterior was a gnawing fear that periodically swept through Janelle's heart. She feared for the future. She feared that life was *too* good, and she knew better than most that nothing lasts forever. Perhaps her insecurity stemmed from a tumultuous childhood, which later led to her parents' divorce. Whatever the reason, Janelle felt undeserving of everything she had. *It'll all come crashing down sooner or later,* she thought. *I hope I can handle it when the clock strikes midnight.*

The way Janelle viewed life, if she could control her surroundings, she could protect her family from hurts and disappointment. So Janelle kept a small circle of friends. *Besides, I'm not an outgoing person, and if fewer people know me, they won't see my character flaws.*

Janelle really believed this. It certainly didn't help matters that she was "just" a housewife. Janelle had noticed that staying home to raise the children—even in the late 1970s—was not held in high esteem by the popular culture. Being a mom wasn't something you wanted to broadcast to the world.

Janelle didn't understand why. She treasured motherhood and could easily understand the value of a mother who was there for her children. But she heard the whispers—and read the articles in women's magazines—that demeaned the choice she'd made to forfeit a career. Thus, she could not shake a feeling of inferiority.

One morning, after the kids had left for school and she had a few minutes to scan the local newspaper, she saw an advertisement for a Positive Thinking Conference. Norman Vincent Peale and Zig Ziglar would be among the slated speakers who would speak at the Indianapolis Convention Center, just minutes from her home.

That's what I need to get me out of these doldrums, she thought. Janelle opened up her closet and took out a gray pin-striped pantsuit with big lapels, just the dressy ticket to be fashionable with all those career types sure to attend this convention.

Janelle had always looked for ways that she could improve herself, better her life. It was for this reason that she was intrigued by the concept of positive thinking that was gaining in popularity in the late 1970s. After taking a seat in the Convention Center—careful not to make eye contact with anyone or draw any untoward attention to herself—Janelle vigorously took notes as speaker after speaker spoke of the importance of having a good attitude.

A fire of enthusiasm began to build in Janelle's soul. Then her focus turned to a courtly man introduced with the alliterative appellation of Zig Ziglar. She quickly turned to a new page in her spiral notebook, ready to capture every word, every morsel of inspiration. But this time, something was different. Spellbound, Janelle quietly released her grip on the pen and set it and the notepad on the floor. She knew there would be no need to take notes because Zig's words were being inscribed in her heart.

What she heard in those next few minutes was indescribable, words of inspiration and hope, like none she had ever heard before, from Zig Ziglar:

> There is an old Bible verse that says, "As ye sow, so also shall ye reap." In the 1970s when computers were coming of age, we frequently heard the term "GIGO," meaning "Garbage In, Garbage Out." You can take that principle to any area of life. We know that whatever we plant in our garden is what we're going to reproduce. When we plant beans, we will raise lots more beans; otherwise, there's no need to plant in the first place.
>
> In an overly simplified version, that's exactly the way the mind works. You are what you are and where you are because of what's gone into your mind: you can change what you are and where you are by changing what goes into your mind. When you plant a negative, you will raise a crop of negatives. When you plant a positive, you will raise a crop of positives. The objective, of course, is to bury all the negatives with a lot of positives.

Janelle understood that she would have to plant many positives since she had been planting many negatives over the years—and reaping a harvest of negativity for a long time. As Zig spoke, she started building on the hope that she had desperately been seeking. A story that inspired her was Zig's one about "Little Johnny."

Little Johnny was a second-grader, and in today's terminology, we would say he was a "pistol." One Friday afternoon the teacher told the class that if anything exciting happened over the weekend, they were to tell the class about it on Monday morning. The following Monday as Little Johnny sat there, he was absolutely beside himself. The teacher could tell something was up.

"Johnny, it looks like you've have a good weekend," remarked the teacher.

"Yes, ma'am, I sure did!" replied the youngster.

"What happened, Johnny?"

"Me and my daddy went fishing, and we caught seventy-five catfish, and they all weighed seventy-five pounds!"

"Now, Johnny, you know that simply is not true."

"Oh, yes, ma'am, it is! My daddy's a great fisherman, and I'm even better than he is. We did catch seventy-five catfish, and they all did weigh seventy-five pounds!"

"Now, Johnny, if I were to tell you that on the way to school this morning a twelve-hundred-pound grizzly bear reared up in front of me and was about to grab me and eat me up when suddenly a little twelve-pound yellow dog jumped up at that grizzly bear, grabbed him by the nose, threw him to the ground, bounced him back and forth, broke his neck and killed him dead, would you believe me?"

"Yes, ma'am, I sure would! As a matter of fact, that's my dog!"

Janelle knew Zig was just telling a story, but she recognized his point: A person with the right attitude—an optimist—has a better chance of making it big in life than someone who walks around looking like the cruise director for the *Titanic*.

Janelle left the Convention Center that day with a new zest for life, realizing that whatever God set before her could be done with honor and joy, even if what happened to be set before her was laundry and dress shirts to be ironed.

While walking to her car, she struck up a conversation with a young woman in her twenties who was accompanied by two men. They had noticed that she had failed to raise her hand when the audience was asked to indicate if they were in sales, marketing or a host of other professions.

"What is it that you do?" asked the woman with a curious voice.

"Why, I'm part of the most honorable profession of them all: I'm a builder of men . . . I'm a mother," replied Janelle.

While the two men watched her walk away with their mouths wide open, the woman almost jumped out of her shoes. "Yes!" she shouted, as she pumped her fist. It was clear to Janelle that there was nothing greater in life than being a mother.

SOMETHING STIRRING INSIDE HER

For the next two years, Janelle underwent an emotional and psychological growth spurt. She was starting to think more positively, and she began writing regularly in a journal, which helped her express and understand the thoughts and feelings that stirred within her soul.

Zig Ziglar was her resource, as Janelle learned to look at herself with new eyes. She could hold her head high. No longer did she feel compelled to apologize for who she was, for being "just a mother." Rather, she was beginning to appreciate the woman God created her to be. When she concentrated on the good things in her life, the negatives diminished. She began to see the advantage of her gentle nature, because it was in the quiet times that great ideas came to her. Janelle's self-esteem grew.

Unfortunately, something else was also growing. One night while lying in bed, she rubbed her left breast with her right hand. Lost in thought, she rubbed it again. Twenty years earlier, her junior high P.E. teacher had taught Janelle's class of adolescent girls how to do a breast self-examination. The mechanics of performing a self-exam came back to her.

As her right hand massaged her breast, something felt unusual. It felt like a lump, but that couldn't be. She had been to the doctor two months earlier for her regular physical exam. No lump had been found. So what was this hard tissue that she was pinching between her fingertips?

Maybe I don't know what a lump is supposed to feel like, she thought. Maybe if I wait a week or two, this thing will go away.

A week came and went. The lump remained in her left breast. Fighting a surge of panic, Janelle picked up the telephone and dialed her doctor. Overnight, it seemed, the fortress of protection that Janelle had so carefully built around her and her family was shattering. Breast cancer? It couldn't be. Janelle Hail did not fit the "profile." Hadn't she taken good care of her body with regular exercise and plenty of fruits and veggies? Wasn't it true that no one in her immediate family had ever experienced breast cancer? And what had she done to deserve this?

Deserved or not, the cancer—a word that actually means "crab-like," she would later learn—had latched itself onto her left breast and would not let go. Doctors said

the best way to arrest the spread of the deadly disease was
to remove the breast.

With great fear, Janelle submitted herself to the life-
changing surgery, and as she came out of the fog of an-
esthesia, her imagination took her to dark and frightful
places. The fears that had lain dormant beneath the surface exploded from within her, spewing out lies and neg-
atively. Although the cancerous growth had been sliced
from her body, images of a disfigured body filled her
mind. Janelle was overwhelmed by thoughts that she would
no longer be loved and that her husband would divorce
her. Life seemed meaningless. How could she be useful to
God again with a broken and marred body?

Even after receiving excellent medical care and a positive prognosis, the fear of death and leaving her precious
children and husband behind tormented her. Janelle
would awake each morning, seemingly refreshed, and then
remember where she was. *Is this the day I'm going to die?* she
would ask herself.

At times, she felt as if she were drowning, but little did
she realize that God, knowing that she would need someone or something to undergird her, had provided the resource that she would need to battle back from this deadly
disease. Now, in her darkest moment, Zig's words and writ-
ings took on an entirely new dimension and became a life
raft in a sea of uncertainty.

One morning, Janelle experienced a turning point in
her life. She realized, once and for all, the power that she
possessed in her mind and will. She moved from a place
of knowing the truth of Zig's words to embracing it. The
truth was planted in her heart and would not leave. What
she did with that truth was up to her.

Janelle began to think about the Scripture that said,

"This is the day the Lord has made. I will rejoice and be glad in it."

With each morning, she whispered those words, and on the fourth morning, something happened inside her. The words flowed out with conviction, and the truth they contained released her from the bondage of fear. *Fear*—not breast cancer—had been her mortal enemy.

Janelle pulled herself out of bed and walked slowly toward the bathroom mirror. She anticipated a struggle, but she knew she would not be fighting this battle alone. She stood in front of the full-length bathroom mirror. She slowly took off her woolen pajamas and stared at her broken body. She dropped her head and softly cried, "Lord, please help me to see myself the way You see me."

FOCUSING ON THE BRIGHT SIDE

That humble cry finally released the anger, hurt and grief that she had dealt with every day since her surgery. An overwhelming feeling of gratitude—yes, gratitude—warmed her heart and calmed her troubled spirit. The eyes of Janelle's soul were opened as she stood before the mirror that morning. She looked at her hands and quietly uttered this prayer: "Thank you, Lord, that I have two hands that work."

Then she looked down at her feet. "Thank you, Lord, that I have two feet to carry me where I need to go."

Then she looked in the mirror. "And thank you, Lord, that I have a mouth to speak of Your goodness, but most of all, that I have a heart to love and help others."

In that moment, God healed her heart. Janelle knew that the cancer was life-threatening, but the fear it generated was not going to stop her from living life unless she wanted it to. She decided to take a positive step, and that first step would lead to her old hairdresser.

As she sat in the chair to have her hair done, Janelle began reading a book given to her by a well-meaning friend. The book was a story of a woman with breast cancer, but as she began turning more and more pages, Janelle became more and more depressed. This wasn't a story of hope, it was about someone embracing death!

Janelle asked her hairdresser to stop snipping for a moment. She stepped out of her chair and tossed the book into a small trash bin filled with hair clippings. With a broad smile of triumph, Janelle then bade the hairdresser to continue. *There's no reason to subject myself to the negative,* she thought. *I will embrace what is good and wholesome.*

As she continued her recovery, Janelle wondered if the way she had lifted herself could help other women suffering from breast cancer. She had always related well to women, so she took a tentative step by volunteering to visit breast cancer victims in the hospital. The more she helped others, the more complete she felt. It wasn't long before others noticed the special touch that Janelle had with women adjusting to mastectomies. She became a sought-after speaker and, over a few years, a recognized authority on breast cancer.

In 1991, Janelle founded the National Breast Cancer Foundation and became its first president. This national outreach to women focuses on education and early detection of breast cancer, which is all-important if one is to beat the disease. The National Breast Cancer Foundation has become an effective clearinghouse of information. Some examples:

- Today, one woman in eight will develop some form of breast cancer. In 1980, that figure was one women in eleven.

- Breast cancer will claim 46,000 women this year.

- Seventy percent of women find their own lumps, as Janelle did, but the best prevention remains breast self-examinations, mammograms and regular doctor visits.

The likelihood that a woman will develop breast cancer is growing, which is why Janelle travels around the country speaking to corporations, women's conferences, homeless shelters and associations about this growing epidemic.

"Zig Ziglar gave me the freedom to dream," she says. "He unlocked my mind to untold possibilities. Never would I have considered founding a nonprofit organization or having the strength to stand up in front of people and say something." Yet Janelle has served as president of the National Speakers Association's Dallas chapter and has won several speaking and writing awards.

A SUNDAY SCHOOL LESSON

While most people consider themselves fortunate to hear Zig Ziglar speak one or two times in their lifetime, Janelle has the opportunity to hear Zig speak just about every Sunday!

Zig leads a Sunday school class at Prestonwood Baptist Church in Dallas, and it shouldn't surprise anyone that the class averages six hundred or so every week—more than many churches in the U.S.

One Sunday morning just before the class was to convene, Janelle stepped into the women's rest room. Just as she entered, Janelle heard a woman say, "Your hair is a mess!"

At first, Janelle thought the woman was talking to her, but then she noticed the woman's four-year-old son standing straight. The mom blithely continued, filling the small rest room with waves of criticism.

"Oh, can't your father do anything right?" she asked, as she roughly smoothed out the boy's hair and Sunday-go-to-meeting clothes. "For land's sake, just look at you. Is that the way you want to go to church?"

The darling, handsome child just stared out into the distance, not saying a word. As the criticism rang in her ears, Janelle couldn't help but be struck by the irony of the situation. Just twenty feet away, one of the most powerful speakers in the world would fill the room with words of life and love. Powerful, positive words.

Janelle washed her hands and walked to the Sunday school class. She took her accustomed seat near the front, then daydreamed while she waited for Zig to begin class. She thought back nearly twenty years to the November day when she was at home recovering from her mastectomy. She looked out her kitchen window and noticed a barren tree in her back yard. Winter was quickly approaching, and all the leaves had fallen to the ground except for one brilliant red leaf that was hanging onto a tree limb with great gusto.

That's the way I want to live, she thought. *I want to hang on to life and love until the very end with everything I've got.*

Janelle Hail has lived a lot of life since those dark times when she wondered if that day would be her last. Like a little red leaf on a gloomy November afternoon, Janelle has hung on for dear life, and she's glad she did.

Ed Hearn

A Major League Test

Ed Hearn waited until his wife departed for work. With the house empty that glum winter morning, he walked downstairs to the basement. It had to be there somewhere. Then he found it—the .357 Magnum handgun his grandfather had given him years earlier.

The gun certainly has some heft, thought Ed, as he tossed it from hand to hand. Ed also weighed his thoughts, which took him further into the abyss of depression. He felt the darkness wrap around him like a heavy blanket. *There really is no way out, is there?*

Ed looked around the basement and quickly found a box of bullets. He slipped a single shell into the chamber. *It can be all over in a manner of moments,* he mused. *All you have to do is lift the gun to your head.* He cocked the hammer.

For ten minutes, Ed contemplated the uncontemplatable. At thirty-three years of age, he thought about meeting his Maker, which gave him pause. *God does not want you to do this,* he reflected. *If you do, He will boot you right out of heaven.*

Then his thoughts turned to his wife, Jill. *I know things didn't work out as planned, baby. You thought you were marrying a rich major league baseball player, and look what you got. We went from the penthouse to the outhouse, didn't we? I was a World Series hero. Now I'm a has-been.* But the idea of leaving Jill behind as a young, childless widow struck him as selfish.

Then Ed recalled having lunch with Zig Ziglar a few months earlier during a Peter Lowe Success Seminar in Kansas City, Missouri.

Zig had closed the morning session with his usual inspirational speech, but Ed had just been Ziglarized in the preceding hour. He just *had* to meet this man. Maybe he would have the right words to beat back the demons of depression that played with his mind.

At the end of his talk, Zig sat on the edge of the stage to meet and greet several hundred seminar attendees who wanted a word or an autograph. Ed hung around the stage, hoping to get Zig's attention while the rest of the crowd filed out of the Kemper Arena to go to lunch. As the throng around Zig dwindled to a half dozen, Ed stepped closer. Ed was an introverted sort, but when he got within earshot of Zig, he blurted out, "Hey, do you have anyone to eat lunch with?"

Zig looked up from the book he was autographing.

"Well, no," replied Zig. "But I've got some things to do. You ought to go have lunch. You need to get back to the next session."

"No, no, no," said Ed. "If you don't have anybody to go to lunch with, I'd love to take you out. There's a great place right down the street."

"Well, if you want to wait for me, stay here where I can see you." Then Zig posed to have his picture taken, and was buttonholed by a woman who poured out her heart for ten minutes.

After a mini counseling session, Zig was finished, and

he and Ed left Kemper Arena for a nearby eatery. When they sat down, Ed expected Zig to talk about himself. Important people have a way of turning the spotlights on themselves, Ed knew, since he had been "important" at one time, too. Instead, Zig quietly asked Ed to tell him his story.

So Ed started at the beginning. Raised in a family that pushed him to excel and produce, Ed became a catcher on the high school baseball team, donning the "tools of ignorance" and dreaming one day of wearing a major league uniform.

Even though he might have gotten three hits in four at-bats, his father would say, "What happened on that fourth one?" instead of "Wow, great job, going three-for-four!" Ed grew up thinking he could never be good enough, even though he earned a 3.96 grade-point average in high school, received a West Point appointment and entertained numerous "free ride" scholarship offers to Ivy League and other major colleges.

Because of his baseball prowess, he was drafted out of high school by the Pittsburgh Pirates, who shipped him out to their farm system. For nearly nine seasons, he toiled in the bush leagues, enduring overnight bus rides and bumpy flights on commuter planes while he chased after a dream. After signing a free-agent contract with the New York Mets, he was finally called up to the parent club in 1986. Ed was now in "The Show," the big leagues. At the age of twenty-six, he had arrived.

The Mets were the "Miracle Mets" that year, and Ed contributed where he could as a backup catcher to Gary Carter. After the Mets won the National League pennant, they squared off against the Boston Red Sox. The Mets were within one out of losing the series in Game 6 when Boston first baseman Bill Buckner let a ground ball to squirt through his legs, allowing the winning run to cross the plate.

When the Mets won Game 7 to complete one of the greatest comebacks in baseball history, Ed charged onto the field and celebrated the Mets' incredible victory before a national TV audience and delirious New York crowd. The club was rewarded with a ticker-tape parade down Broadway, and a month later, Ed stood with his teammates in the Rose Garden and accepted the accolades of President Reagan in a White House reception for the team.

A TRADE-OFF

In the blink of an eye, that all changed. Following the '86 season, he was traded to the Kansas City Royals for pitcher David Cone. Ed was expected to be the cornerstone of the Royals' rebuilding plan, and if he had a couple of good years with the Kansas City club, he could sign one of those fat long-contracts worth millions of dollars. He would never have to work again if he chose not to.

Then Ed suffered a terrible rotator cuff injury to his right shoulder, which limited his effectiveness behind the plate and in the batting box. For three years he struggled to piece together a comeback, even returning to the minor leagues. He endured surgeries, rehabs and the barbs of sports talk-show hosts who called the Ed Hearn–for–David Cone trade the "worst in Royals history."

That hurt, but try as he might, his career was finished, and in the spring of 1991, Ed was not in some Florida spring training camp but embarking on a job search in the real world. The new developments certainly put a strain on his marriage. He had met Jill during the Mets' championship run, and they married in 1987.

The time for fun and games was over. Although Ed was leaving baseball with a bad taste in his mouth, he had a good head on his shoulders. Before he joined the New York Mets, he had completed two years of college. *I shouldn't have too much trouble finding something I can do,* he thought. Ed underwent a battery of career tests, looking for a good match. The results stated:

- He wanted to work with people.

- He wanted to be his own boss.

- He wanted to have flexible hours.

Ed turned to the insurance field. The New York Life Insurance Company wanted this former player, so they placed him in a training program that included listening to tapes from some guy named Zig Ziglar. He may have popped one into his car's cassette player, but it didn't stay in there long. *I know hype when I hear it,* Ed thought. *I don't need all that stuff. Besides, I was in the big leagues. I'm macho, got what it takes.*

Six months into his insurance career, however, Ed came down with three potentially deadly diseases in the span of a calendar year. His kidneys were in terrible shape, so doctors ordered daily dialysis, along with monthly $2,500 blood infusion treatments. Then he developed a gamma globulin deficiency, which was treated by ingesting thirty-four pills a day. When his body still did not respond, doctors performed a kidney transplant. Now he had to take more drugs to prevent his body from rejecting the new kidney.

All these medications caused delirious side effects, including depression and mood swings. It didn't help matters when Ed developed severe sleep apnea, a condition in which the body stops breathing while sleeping, thus sparking thrashing and gasping for air. By early 1993, Ed was living in a perpetual state of fatigue, going from treatment to treatment, sleeping with a breathing machine, and wondering how he would ever pay for medication that was costing him $50,000 a year. Ed was one depressed dude.

Zig quietly listened as Ed recounted this story. One of Zig's saying is that when you meet people, treat them as if they are facing challenges, because 90 percent of the time they are. But Zig knew that wasn't what Ed Hearn needed to hear. Instead, Zig leaned over the table and said, "You can change where you are in life by changing what you put in your mind."

Ed felt as if he had been hit over the head by a poleax. Zig's words stuck in his mind like pine tar sticks to a major league bat, and those words of wisdom came back to him six months later when he held the .357 Magnum in the palm of his right hand. *You can change where you are in life by changing what you put in your mind.* It was then that Ed knew he didn't want to put a bullet into his brain. He wanted something else: the will to continue, the desire to take one step at a time, and the chance to make something more out of his life and marriage.

Ed put the gun down. He opened the chamber and pulled out the unspent bullet. Right then and there, he made a conscious decision to go on with life. He wasn't sure what he was going to do, but he was going to do something. *You can change where you are in life by changing what you put in your mind.*

Ed decided to do three things. The first was get back to the basics of his beliefs, his faith. He began reading the Bible, discovering areas of solace and comfort that only God's Word can bring to a hurting heart. "Come to me, all you who are weary and burdened, and I will give you rest," said Jesus in Matthew 11:28–30. "Take my yoke upon you and learn from me, for I am gentle and humble in heart, and you will find rest for your souls. For my yoke is easy and my burden is light." Ed also began praying and hanging around with other Christian people who could love and support him.

Then he sought professional help. That was hard. "Get help? Come on. I was a professional athlete. I was raised by parents who told me that you don't go outside the family for help," said Ed. "That was the worst."

After seeing a psychologist, Ed purchased a Ziglar tape series and began listening religiously. "It just became a way of life," he said. "I would listen everywhere I went in the car, and I could feel the difference it was making mentally in me because I was putting positive things in place of all the negative thoughts I had."

A LOCAL TALK

Not long after the incident in the basement, Ed was asked to speak to the Rotary Club in Kansas City by a former Chiefs player. *Just do the old jock talk at the local civic club,* he thought. Ed didn't want to disappoint his friend, so he accepted the invitation.

But Ed took a chance that afternoon. Instead of

describing what it was like to win a World Series, he stood before the lunchtime crowd and told his story—the story you're reading. Afterward, a man came up and handed him a business card. "Ed, you have a great story, and you tell it well," said the man. "Corporate America will pay you to do this. They need people like you because they're facing great challenges out there today."

Wow. Maybe this is what it's all about, he thought. *Maybe the platform that I had as a professional athlete has paled in comparison to what has been built for me through all this adversity.*

A seed had been planted. Ed continued to work with the tapes and seek clinical help with his depression. Then one day he picked up the business card he had been handed at that Rotary Club luncheon. It was from Brad Plum, president of the National Speakers Bureau. He dialed the number and said, "Brad, I'd like to talk to you about what you said to me that day."

Brad offered to help Ed get started and in 1994 he was asked to speak eighteen times. The following year it jumped to thirty-five. By 1996, he was up to fifty or so, and these days, Ed speaks nearly two hundred times a year in front of audiences seeking a dose of encouragement.

"I'm a miniature Zig now," beamed Ed. "I have the opportunity to touch people's lives, and what can be better than that? One of the things I try to do when I'm out there is stick around and talk to people when I'm done. So many speakers blow into meetings, do their thing, and hop in their car or limo and boom, they're out of there. You're not just getting a speaker with Ed Hearn. You're getting a person that people will be able to spend time with.

"And invariably, people will come up to me and begin

sharing on an individual, one-on-one basis—just like that day when Zig sat on the Kemper Arena stage and listened to people tell him about their lives.

"That's something I've always tried to do, because I know how much that meant to me the day I sat there in the auditorium. Zig could have run off that day. But he stayed and made himself available to me and to others. It's a far-fetched dream to think I could ever become a Zig Ziglar, but I certainly think I have the opportunity to impact many thousands of lives by and continuing to do what I do today.

"So many people, especially celebrities or these big-time speakers, don't have time to make time. But Zig Ziglar did. He's a model for what I'm trying to be today."

Ed Hearn has also written an excellent book called Conquering Life's Curves, *which details his struggles in and out of the game. Each chapter contains an "Inside Pitch" box that helps the reader live a championship life.*

Linda Warner

Back from the Brink

Linda Warner doesn't remember much of her mother, a single-parent mom who gave birth to her at twenty years of age. Her mother rented an apartment above a San Francisco bar, and whenever she wanted to get sauced—which was often—she locked Linda in a closet and walked downstairs to have a few drinks.

Although Linda's father had left just before she was born, when he found out his daughter was being shunted to a closet, he filed for divorce and received full custody. Linda was two years old when her father came to take her away.

Dad, unfortunately, was an alcoholic, too. He didn't know much about how to raise a child, so he fed her Twinkies and Sugar Pops for breakfast, lunch, and dinner. The sugar overload led to Linda's long struggle with her weight. When she started school and began to learn more about the world around her, she envied other kids who had a mother and a father, some money, and a better start in life. Linda was always down on herself.

When Linda was seven years old, things went from bad to worse. Her father remarried and his new wife had two teenage children from a previous marriage. When Linda's dad was away on business, which happened quite frequently, they would torment her, one time even tying her up in a chair and poking her with hairbrushes.

One day her father came home early from work and discovered what they were doing to her. He took her away to live at her grandmother's house, but he continued to live with his wife and her teenage children. Linda had a hard time understanding that.

Linda's grandmother was a positive influence in her life, but she died a year after Linda arrived. With no other options, Linda moved back in with her father, and thankfully he subsequently left his wife.

When Linda started maturing, her father was clueless about the changes she was experiencing during puberty. Linda didn't comprehend the physical changes either, and without a parent to turn to, she hid a bra at a friend's house because she was too embarrassed to talk to Dad about it. When she dared look at her body in the mirror, she felt shamed at what she saw. She hated herself.

Her self-hatred led to thoughts about dying. For some reason, Linda began believing, that she was going to die on a Sunday, so she would ask friends in the neighborhood if she could go to church with them. She thought that maybe being in a church would put off her inevitable death. She didn't know anything about religion or God, but she felt church had a mysterious power that could somehow save her.

Linda married at nineteen, not because she loved the guy, but because she wanted to escape her dismal existence with her father. Predictably, the teen marriage lasted only long enough for Linda to bring two children into this world. When the union broke up, she needed a job and started working for a supermarket chain.

She started her career in the supermarket industry by bagging groceries as a teenager and pushing heavy carts to the parking lot for quarter tips. From there, she stocked shelves at 4 A.M. and learned how to watch for candy theft at the checkout lines. It took Linda Warner seventeen long years to work her way up the supermarket ladder—not an easy climb in a male-dominated profession—into a management position. During that time she met and married her present husband, Tim. Life was finally looking up for Linda, she had a happy marriage, a wonderful family, and a promising career. In fact, life seemed perfect that summer day when her family decided to go on an outing to Lake Sonoma. She and her husband, along with his two brothers and her twenty-five-year-old daughter, Stacy (born from her first marriage), jumped in their small motorboat to fish for some of the bass that Lake Sonoma was known for. As they skimmed along the glassy waters, Linda commented that Stacy, seven months pregnant with her first child, was a trooper to come along.

They trolled into a small cove and let the engine die. Linda saw families swimming in the brisk water near the shoreline. Above her, several osprey—huge birds with wingspans of six feet—squawked as they circled the lake. Tim brought the skiff under a barren tree just as the ospreys alighted on one of the tree's branches.

Suddenly the sound of wood snapping caused the boaters to look skyward. Tim sensed the danger first; he dove headlong into the lake as a heavy branch dropped toward the motorboat. One of Linda's brothers-in-law covered his head with his hands, while the other one ducked. Linda instinctively leaped on top of her daughter to protect her, but then her world went black.

When she regained consciousness, her husband and inlaws were lifting a large branch off her lower back. Apparently the ospreys had come to rest on a dead tree, and the branch could not support their weight.

As Linda moaned in pain from the terrible injuries, the family rushed her to a nearby emergency room. At first, the ER doctors thought she had broken her back, but two CAT scans indicated that this was not the case.

"Can I go back to work?" Linda asked, since she was in the midst of important management training. She knew she *had* to be at work the next day.

"If you take it easy and feel up to it, there's no reason why you can't," a doctor told her.

The next day, Linda's shift nearly killed her. She knew her injuries were more than harmless bumps and bruises. She went to see an orthopedic surgeon, who ordered more X rays. The doctor found a broken vertebrae and two ruptured disks.

The news devastated Linda. "How come the emergency room doctors didn't tell me that?" she asked the doctor.

"The original CAT scans must not have been taken low enough on your back," the surgeon replied, not wanting to criticize another professional's work.

"Oh. So what can be done?"

"Nothing," he replied. "You'll want to rest and recuperate, of course, but there's basically nothing we can do for you."

"But what about my pain?"

"We can take care of that. I'll write up a prescription."

Over the next few months, Linda visited doctor after doctor, each one giving her more pills than the last. But the excruciating pain remained. She was forced to take a medical leave from work. After four months without improvement, Linda visited yet another orthopedic surgeon. He suggested a lamenectomy—shaving the disks and pushing the nerves back up.

"Let's go for it," she said.

The tricky surgery was successful. Linda began physical therapy, knowing that she had to get back to work soon or start looking for another job.

Linda didn't know it, but she was being perceived as a liability to the supermarket chain for several reasons: She was a woman; she was older than forty; and she was coming off a debilitating injury that limited her physical ability to do the job. Upon her return, she was transferred to a different store; it was the one employees begged to get transferred out of, with a manager the workers nicknamed "Hatchet Man." To add insult to injury, she was assigned to work the 3 A.M. to noon shift. She was told that part of her new duties was to perform all the price changes, an onerous task usually shared by five to seven clerks. The work was physically difficult because Linda was five-foot, two-inches tall, yet many of the price changes were on the highest and lowest shelves, meaning she was constantly reaching and bending.

In the gloom of night and into the bright morning hours, Linda swept through the entire store, changing hundreds of prices in every department, willing her damaged body to finish the shift. She was so sore that when she arrived home from her first day back on the job, her daughter had to assist her out of the car. The next day, Linda could hardly move, so she called in sick. The employer's response: "You're fired!"

She no longer had a job, but her back pain still remained. Linda sought more medical answers, and a new doctor suggested fusing two disks in her back. Reluctantly she submitted to the surgery, but coming out, the pain never relaxed its grip. She couldn't function at all.

Medication made the pain somewhat bearable but this was no way to live. Linda, never one to give up, visited yet another doctor, and after taking more X-rays he made a surprising discovery. Linda's disks had been fused on one side and not the other. No wonder she couldn't get out of bed!

"I have more bad news for you," the doctor said. "I'm afraid you will have to undergo a third back operation."

Linda felt like her world was spinning out of control. She was out of a job, in constant pain, dependent on medication, and overwhelmed by mounting medical bills. Now she was being told that her last surgery contributed to her agony and she would have to undergo the procedure again.

With no other choice, Linda submitted to back surgery for the third time. The doctors attempted another fusion. She was told that the procedure was successful, but the recovery was long and the pain lingered.

Linda was at the end of her rope. The feelings of self-hatred and despair from her youth began to resurface. She fell face-first into a black hole of depression.

ZIG PULLS HER OUT

During her recuperation, Linda's family and friends rallied around her and forced her to keep going. Although she would rather have spent her days in bed, Linda was often called on by concerned relatives or taken out to visit friends. It was during one of these visits that she noticed a tape series sitting on her friend's table. She inquired about them and her friend told her that it was a Zig Ziglar series.

"Who's he?" Linda asked.

"He's a wonderful inspirational speaker."

If anyone could use some inspiration, it's me, she thought.

"Could I borrow those tapes?"

Linda listened and listened, fascinated by what Zig Ziglar had to say. His motivational stories touched something inside her, his words of encouragement seemed to be directed right at her. Best of all, he made her think—about who she was, what she wanted, and who she could be.

The tapes caused her to recall painful childhood memories and realize that those negative experiences shaped her life. But Zig also helped her recognize that she could take control and reshape her life. That's when Linda decided to fill her mind with positive thoughts. She could have fixated on the fact that she was forty-five years old, overweight, physically disabled through no fault of her own and practically bankrupt. Instead she would focus on all the wonderful things she had: her family, her friends and the ability to turn her life around. As Zig said, it was never too late to start on the road back.

Zig's teachings also took her down an unexpected path. Many times when she was listening to Zig, she would think, *I understand and agree with everything he is saying, but I feel like I'm missing a piece of the puzzle. What am I missing?*

And then one afternoon it came to her. *Zig is talking about God.* Although Linda found solace in church when she was a young girl, she never really experienced God.

Maybe that's what I need in my life: Maybe it is God who can see me through this.

Linda desperately wanted to explore this new idea, and she asked family members and friends to go to church with her. Her sister-in-law agreed to go.

"Which church should we go to?" she asked.

Linda shrugged her shoulders, so they pulled out the Saturday newspaper and decided Linda would pick one this week and her sister-in-law would pick one the following week.

Linda chose Calvary Community Church, which happened to be meeting in a theater, not a church. That unusual venue didn't bother Linda. When she walked in, she knew that was the place she wanted to be.

That first Sunday the pastor preached out of a Bible, which fascinated Linda. She knew nothing about the Bible, so afterward she visited a Christian bookstore, which had dozens to choose from. Linda was overwhelmed. When she asked the clerk for advice, she said, "Well, we have the New American Standard Bible and the New International Version and the King James Revised Standard and the . . ."

"No, I just want a Bible," Linda interrupted, and she chose an NIV Student Bible because the English looked easy to understand.

Since then, Linda has been baptized, and now she's the co-director of the church nursery. She says it feels great to be needed and available to serve in the church.

Not long ago, Linda heard that Zig Ziglar was going to be speaking in San Jose as part of the Peter Lowe Success Seminar. She had to see this man in person and Linda was not disappointed. When she heard Zig speak, she became truly inspired by him. In fact, she was inspired to return to school, where she took a class in child development at Santa Rosa Junior College.

Linda felt good until she took the first test. When the teacher handed her test back Linda saw the big, fat D in the corner, swept up her books and ran to her car.

She took several deep breaths. *If you leave now, you will never do this again,* she thought. She slowed down. *Think. Think What would Zig do? I know; he'd give it another try.*

Linda screwed up her courage and sought out a counselor. She should at least talk to someone before she decided school wasn't right for her.

"Let me tell you a little something," said the counselor. "You wouldn't believe how many people come back to school and think they've got it made because they have all this wisdom and experience. But schoolwork is different, and there's often a rude awakening."

The counselor encouraged her to give it another try.

"I don't know if I can go back into that classroom," she sniffled, but she agreed to think it over. Later that day, she called the teacher.

"I'm the one who ran out of the classroom yesterday," she began. "I was so embarrassed by my grade. I felt like a failure, but I do want to continue taking the class."

The teacher said, "Good, I'm glad you're coming back. I'll work with you in whatever way you need."

That's when Linda's determination set in. In the past, she would have walked away, but thanks to Zig Ziglar, she knew the steps she had to take. On the next three tests, Linda made As.

"This is what Zig Ziglar has meant to me," she said. "It doesn't matter who I am, where I've been, or what I was born into, I can do anything I put my mind to."

Clint Lewis

He Lost His Sight—But Found His Vision

One of Clint Lewis's best childhood memories transpired during an elementary school wrestling meet. Clint, a third-grader at the time, had won several preliminary bouts and was about to wrestle in the championship round.

His parents and older brother and younger sister, plus classmates and their families, cheered from the bleachers as the referee blew his whistle to start the match. Clint placed his arms in front of him and started to warily circle his opponent. He was looking for a "hand hold," in which the wrestlers lock hands, then use their strength to maneuver for better position.

Suddenly, Clint found the hands of his opponent and quickly grabbed hold, then spun his classmate to the mat. "Two points," barked the referee, as Clint wrapped his right arm around his opponent's waist and tried to flip him so he could work for the pin.

For several minutes, the two third-graders grappled each other, Clint looking to pin the other boy's shoulders and his opponent searching for an escape. The small crowd yelled encouragement as the seconds ticked off the clock.

The buzzer rang, signaling the end of the match. Clint stood up and took his position next to the referee, who held hands with each wrestler. When he raised Clint's arm into the air, his family and friends burst into applause and rushed to the mat to congratulate the young boy for winning the third-grade championship.

He felt several pats on the back. "Atta-boy, Clint," bellowed one father. "Way to go!" His parents hugged and whispered their congratulations into his ear. Clint felt fantastic, as proud as any eight-year-old boy could at a moment like that.

I wish I could see my parents' faces right now, he thought. *That would be even more special than winning this wrestling tournament.*

You see, Clint Lewis was blind, a victim of glaucoma.

A WORLD WITHOUT SIGHT

Clint was two years old when he went to an eye doctor for an important exam. His parents already knew that he had glaucoma, a disease of the eye characterized by a hardening of the eyeballs that eventually leads to blindness.

The eye doctor dilated Clint's pupils and peered inside, checking his diagnosis.

"Mrs. Lewis," he said, motioning the nervous mother to come closer. "Mrs. Lewis, I'm afraid I have bad news," he announced, as young Clint heard every word. "The glaucoma has made your son blind, and there is no hope that he will regain his sight in his lifetime. My advice to you is to just treat him like any other child. Don't pamper him, or you will raise a very wimpy boy."

Mrs. Lewis took the advice to heart. When it came time for Clint to enter kindergarten, local school authorities in

North Salt Lake, Utah, said Clint had to attend the district's School for the Blind.

Mrs. Lewis would have none of it. She believed that Clint would not only learn more in regular school, but he also needed to learn how to be "social" with the sighted world. Blind schools, she had heard, didn't socialize their students well.

"If you went to a blind school, they treated you like a blind student," said Clint. "If you went to a public school, they treated you like a regular student. That's why my parents insisted I attend a 'regular' school just like any other child in the neighborhood."

The school district, however, had another view. "Your son must attend the School for the Blind," school authorities insisted.

"No, he won't," replied Mrs. Lewis, who took the school district to court and won her bid to keep Clint in regular classes. Mrs. Lewis was also determined to keep her home as "normal" as possible. That meant Clint made his own peanut-butter-and-jelly sandwiches for his school lunch, just like his siblings. That meant Clint cleaned up the dinner dishes and vacuumed the house, just like his siblings. "My mom and dad treated me as if I was a sighted boy," he said. "I had to do my chores, and I couldn't use my blindness as an excuse."

Clint started wrestling in second grade. His opponents quickly learned that if they snuck in behind him, they could wrap their arms around Clint and make a takedown. So the coach adjusted the rules: Clint and his opponent had to keep touching hands so Clint would "know" where his opponent was. If the two adversaries ever stopped touching hands for too long, the ref would blow his whistle.

"In some ways, it was an advantage being a blind wrestler," said Clint. "I could use my sense of feel and tell when someone's balance was off, then go for the takedown."

Clint excelled on the wrestling mat throughout his school years, even competing in high school. After graduation, he left home and moved out on his own. "I thought I was independent," said Clint. "I used a white cane to get around, but it was pretty hard. While tapping my cane on the sidewalk, it would get caught, nearly pole-vaulting me into the air. After I talked to my parents about it, we decided to get me a guide dog, whom I named Libo. He's a yellow labrador, and he's made such a difference in my life. He keeps me on the sidewalk and doesn't cross the street until it's safe. He helps me find doors. He knows the difference between right and left. We can travel on just about anything—trains, planes and buses."

In his early twenties, Clint took a job as an exercise therapist at a work activity center for the mentally handicapped. His job was to help adults and youngsters learn to use their motor skills better. He also taught blind kids and adults how to use a cane. In the winter months, he coached wrestling at a junior high school.

Clint also harbored dreams of someday having his name in lights. He liked to play the guitar and sing, and when times were slow at the activity center, he unpacked his guitar and entertained the clients. He talked in between songs about what was in his heart.

"At the activity center I was helping people, but I didn't feel like I was helping *a lot* of people," said Clint. "I felt like it was a dead-end job. There was no opportunity for advancement, and my self-esteem was low. I dreamed of what I could do next, but I never thought I could ever make that dream a reality.''

His older brother, Jeff, dropped by his apartment one afternoon, sensing his brother needed a pick-me-up. Jeff was an independent Amway distributor, and part of his training included listening to a Zig Ziglar tape series.

"You've got to hear Zig Ziglar," said Jeff. "You will really enjoy his energy."

Sounds good enough for me, thought Clint. Listening to tapes would be a good way to pass the hours after work.

Now, imagine that you are blind and that you are listening to Zig Ziglar for the first time. You listen differently than sighted persons. You don't have visual distractions like newspapers or magazines. You're able to concentrate and hear inflections and pauses in ways that sighted people cannot. That's because you are relying solely on your sense of hearing—a sense that's been honed over the years to make up for your loss of sight.

The first time Clint listened to Zig Ziglar on tape, he was captivated by his smooth cadence and honey-on-bread delivery. "Zig Ziglar spoke with a truth and honesty that was absolutely compelling to me," said Clint. "There was no doubting the sincerity in his voice."

Clint loved Zig's "bullfrog" story. "Zig told the story of a down-home boy saying, 'Friend, if you've got to swallow a bullfrog, you just don't want to look at that sucker too long. He ain't gonna get no purtier! As a matter of fact, the longer you look, the uglier he gets.' Zig said that's the way unpleasant tasks are. What Zig taught me is that even if you don't want to do something but you know you should do it, then you should it. It's that plain and simple."

Another Zig truism caught Clint's ear: "You can have everything in life you want if you will just help enough other people get what they want."

That statement changed Clint's thinking about working at the activity center. Overnight he started doing as much as he could. When coaching the junior high wrestlers, his workouts became a lot more than takedowns and reversals. "I began teaching the kids to believe in themselves," said Clint, "and at the end of every practice, I would have the team lie down on the mat and listen to Zig talk on tape. Zig has a way of breaking down his concepts so that even seventh- and eighth-graders can understand what he is saying."

SEEING THE ROAD AHEAD

As Clint lay on the mat with his wrestlers one afternoon, he decided then and there that he wanted to become the next Zig Ziglar. Well, maybe not *the* next Zig Ziglar, but he wanted to teach others to believe in themselves.

While he kept his day job, Clint took small steps toward building a speaking career. Where to start? *Well, I seem to have a good touch with kids. I know. I could talk to little kids in day-care centers,* he thought.

So he made up a flier and began passing it around at day-care centers in the Salt Lake City area. He quickly discovered that he had to tailor his message to the audience, and preschoolers weren't about to sit still and listen to a blind person talk for twenty minutes about believing in themselves.

So Clint opened his heart on what it was like to be

blind, showing the three-year-olds alphabet cards in Braille and how to use a white cane. Then he would introduce Libo and describe what his guide dog could do for him.

"Then I would play a few songs for the kids," said Clint. The children loved him.

Clint continued to build his speaking avocation, day-care center by day-care center. The only way he could get around Salt Lake City, however, was by public transportation—the city bus—which made life rather tricky.

In the morning he would call the day-care center and tell them he was on his way, and then board a bus near his home. With the day-care center address in hand, he would ask the driver which line to transfer to or where his stop was. All too often, however, he would be dropped off five or six blocks away from the center with no clue of how to get there.

As a blind person, Clint had accepted long ago that he needed help from others, so he wasn't too proud to knock on doors or ask strangers for directions. Many people chose to either drive him or walk him to the day-care center.

Yes, he worried for his safety on occasion, but he figured there were more good people out there than bad. He had also learned from Zig to concentrate on the positive. He remembered hearing Zig ask listeners to place masking tape on the bathroom mirror, then write down goals or attitudes to strive for on the tape. "Zig wanted us to wake up thinking, *I'm a champ; I can do this,*" said Clint, "and not start the day by saying to ourselves, *I've got another boring day to get through.* Zig called this having good 'self-talk.' "

Of course, Clint knew he would never see masking tape on his bathroom mirror, but he could ensure that his "self-talk"—the thoughts running through his mind—was positive.

For instance, if his goal was to speak at three day-care centers each day, then he needed to take baby steps to get there. "I broke my goals down by telling myself that if I wanted to get three day-care centers, I had to make twenty phone calls. So I did that."

One afternoon a father came to see Clint speak at his child's day care, and he was impressed with the way Clint handled himself. The father, an agent who booked speakers for school assemblies, approached Clint and commented that if he could come up with a more "motivational-type talk," then he was sure he could book him into schools throughout Utah and the rest of the country, if that was what Clint wanted to do.

Want to do? Are you kidding?

Every day became an adventure for the young man. To travel from city to city he relied on Greyhound Bus. When he told the driver where he was going, the driver would often reply, "Okay, there's no bus stop in town, so we will have to drop you off on the freeway." The bus would come to a halt, the door would swing open, and Clint would hear the driver say, "The town is about a mile to your right. Good luck."

And then he and Libo would get a good whiff of diesel exhaust.

What did Clint do? What he'd always done—put one foot forward at a time. "I would think, *What am I going to do? I can't turn back.* Libo and I would go forward, and eventually Libo would see some lights on at a house, and he would lead me to the front door. I would tell whoever answered that I was blind and that the bus driver had dropped me off on the Interstate. Most of the time, people would offer to drive me to a nearby motel."

Clint has experienced some frustrating moments on the road. Once in Montana he was staying in a tiny hotel in the dead of winter. Clint met some nice folks in the hotel lobby, and before too long he had his guitar out, and they sang songs until midnight. Then they all left for their rooms. Clint reached into his pocket but his room key wasn't there. He walked to his room, but it was locked. Back in the lobby he yelled for help, but no one came.

Frustrated, feeling sorry for himself, he slept with Libo on a cold couch in the lobby. That night he decided he was going to go home. Traveling was too difficult for him. When he woke up, the hotel staff apologized profusely and offered to drive him to the school where he was scheduled to speak. "That was my toughest time," said Clint. "I wanted to pack it in, but I gathered up the courage to keep going."

PASTIMES

A couple of years ago, Clint was back home in a pub, where he likes to play darts. You may wonder how a blind person plays darts, and this is how Clint does it: He asks a couple of people to walk up to the dartboard and begin talking. Then he tells them to move and he throws where he heard the talking.

"Actually, I'm a pretty good dart player," said Clint, who met a young newspaper editor in Salt Lake City named Tracy Thompson through a dart-playing friend. They have become inseparable and plan to marry. Meanwhile, Tracy quit her newspaper job to go on the road with Clint and now drives him to his various speaking engagements, which average three or four school assemblies a day, or about 450 a year.

"Tracy believes in me and what we're doing," said Clint, who recently turned thirty. "She's been a big help driving me on the road nine months a year, racking up more than forty thousand miles. She's just as much a part of this as I am. We're a great team together."

But there's also one other thing you should know about Clint Lewis: He likes to skydive and bungee jump.

Bungee jump? A blind person?

Yes, and when a *Good Morning, America* producer heard about it, they did a feature story on the blind bungee jumper who likes to sing and speak to school-age children.

"I know this sounds funny coming from a blind guy, but I have a fear of heights. Obviously, I can't see what's down there, but I needed to challenge this fear and beat it," said Clint. "And that's what I tell kids: We need to challenge and beat our fears. If we can do that, we feel better about ourselves and develop more confidence.

"There's another thing I always say: 'When you wake up in the morning, don't wonder if today is going to be a good day. When you wake up in the morning, *make* today a good day, and you do that by having a good attitude.' "

Then Clint finishes his talk by singing, "I Can See Clearly Now."

Clint Lewis frequently speaks to corporate audiences as well. For more information, call (801) 424-1766.

Kim Whitham

Guilt That Washed Away

Kim Whitham's battle with guilt started when she was in first grade.

Seven-year-old Kim was skipping alongside a dam near her Kansas home with her father and brother Marty, who was just a year younger than she. No one saw the rattlesnake as it slid across the dirt path toward the unsuspecting family. Snakes were not unheard of on the Kansas prairie, but many were harmless and not poisonous.

Not this rattler.

In an instant, the snake struck, sinking its saberlike teeth into Marty's leg and injecting its lethal venom into muscle and bone.

Marty shrieked in pain. Kim, meanwhile, just stood there, too frightened to move. Her father grabbed the snake and tried to jerk it off Marty's leg, but the snake would not let go, probably because its fangs were sunk into the bone. Meanwhile, deadly venom continued to be introduced into Marty's bloodstream. Finally, Kim's father stood on the snake and yanked its jaw from Marty's leg. Then he started sprinting for the house with Marty in his arms.

The nearest city hospital was in Ulysses, Kansas, a half-hour drive. Compounding matters, the region was being hit by a terrible dirt storm. They packed Marty's leg in ice as the doctor had instructed, and a neighbor held Marty in the car and put his belt around the leg as a tourniquet. The doctor had warned them they only had thirty minutes to get him there.

Other neighbors and the family jumped in the family car and headed out, but on the way to the hospital, they experienced a blowout. They didn't want to take the time to change the tire, so they rolled into a farmhouse and began honking. A man and his son ran out to see what was going on, and the son told everyone to pile into his car. As they sped down the highway, Kim's parents knew they were in a race to save their son's life.

It's all my fault, Kim thought. *If I had seen the snake, Marty wouldn't have been bitten. Why didn't it bite me?*

Doctors at Bob Wilson Memorial Hospital in Ulysses worked heroically to keep Marty alive. Anti-venom vaccine had to be rushed by state troopers from Garden City and Liberal because enough wasn't on hand. The ER staff stabilized the boy, but they had to keep his leg frozen in ice because every time they unpacked his leg from the ice, his heart threatened to stop.

After a few weeks in the hospital, Marty had to be flown by a local farmer to Kansas City. Gangrene had set in on the boy's right leg, so to save his life, doctors had to amputate the leg above the knee and graft a large area of skin so he would have a stump on which to wear a wooden leg. The skin grafting sites all got staph infection, however, and Marty would beg for morphine shots to ease the terrible pain.

After the amputation, life became contentious around

Kim's household. Her parents began fighting with each other. When Dad yelled at Mom (or vice versa), another wave of guilt swept over Kim. *It's all my fault*, she thought. *Why didn't the snake bite me?*

LEAVING HOME

Kim moped through much of elementary school, and she and Marty became emotionally distanced from each other. Perhaps it was because whenever she looked at her brother, she saw him walking on his wooden leg and she blamed herself for his condition.

When Kim was thirteen, she and a fellow classmate named Jeff Whitham started going out with each other. Perhaps she needed Jeff to fill a hole in her life. Kim and Jeff were nearly inseparable through high school, and even though they attended different colleges, they were only ninety minutes apart. The courtship continued.

Kim was majoring in an executive secretarial program at the Brown Mackie College in Salina, Kansas, but being on her own could not dispel the dark clouds of depression that periodically swept over her. Her unending guilt over her brother continued to plague her and kept her from fully enjoying college life. One course she liked was a business class. The instructor did interesting things like play a tape series from some guy named Zig Ziglar.

"You're really going to like listening to these tapes," said the instructor. "Zig Ziglar is great at motivating people."

Great, I can use some of that, thought Kim. *I'm always down in the dumps.*

One of Kim's favorite "Zig stories" was the one about John Marshall, because it made such an important point.

In 1848, John Marshall unearthed some gravel in Sutter's Creek in northern California and glimpsed glittering pebbles and stones. Gold! News of the gold strike spread like wildfire.

People from all over the world stopped everything to set out for the gold fields of California: The Gold Rush of 1849 was on. Many fortunes were made as miners laid claim to wealth they had come seeking. Meanwhile, prosperous towns sprang up with dry goods, grocery stores, lumber mills and a host of other businesses. Like most stories, however, this one has its share of disappointments. There were the usual "sharks" who hovered around and took advantage of some of the newcomers, which wasn't a pretty sight.

One of the ironies of the story, however, was that in the late 1870s, in an abandoned mine shaft, the body of an itinerant miner was found. His papers revealed that he was John Marshall—the man who discovered the gold back in 1848. Unfortunately, Mr. Marshall had failed to stake his own claim.

The sad story of John Marshall is true for many people because, in a metaphorical sense, there is a gold mine anywhere we go. The geographical location has very little to do with it—it's there wherever you might be. I've seen prosperity in desolate areas, and I have seen poverty in flourishing areas. What I've learned is that it's not really the territory; it's the individual.

The reality is that all of us are born to win, but to be the winners we were born to be, we've got to "stake our claim." We've got to claim the abilities we have and apply those abilities wherever we might be.

"The John Marshall story told me that I had potential—potential to be a person of great worth," said Kim. "That helped keep me going, especially during the times I battled depression."

While still in college, Kim, then twenty years old, married Jeff after seven years of dating. Within a couple of years of their wedding, however, Jeff began experiencing terrible intestinal cramps, bouts of nausea and nonstop diarrhea.

After a week of tests, doctors determined that Jeff was suffering from Crohn's disease, an inflammatory bowel condition.

What is Crohn's disease? Crohn's disease is a chronic inflammatory bowel disease. It can affect any portion of the digestive tract, but it typically affects the small intestine and/or the colon. Symptoms include vomiting, fever, night sweats, loss of appetite, general feeling of weakness, severe abdominal cramps and diarrhea.

As the Whithams began dealing with this news, Kim was pregnant with their first child. The pregnancy was not an easy one. Their son was born a month premature and was not breathing upon arrival. Doctors administered oxygen to him, but years later, the family learned that the oxygen had caused one of his eyes not to function properly. After two days at home, severe jaundice set in, then seizures began racking his tiny body.

The baby was rushed to intensive care in Wichita, where the family learned he was an ideal candidate for SIDS—sudden infant death syndrome. Because his heart and breathing would start and stop periodically, he had to be put on a monitor for a year. Finally, he developed severe asthma, which has plagued him his entire life.

Twinges of guilt seeped into Kim's mind. *Didn't I do*

everything that a first-time mom is supposed to do? she asked herself night after sleepless night.

After Kim gave birth to a second boy, nearly four years later, she and Jeff wanted a third child. The third pregnancy went fairly well, but when Kim was full-term, the unborn baby stopped moving. Waves of panic rose in Kim's throat as she rushed to the hospital, where an ultrasound confirmed that the baby was dead. An emergency C-section was performed.

Lying in her hospital bed, Kim had never felt more worthless. *The baby's death is my fault,* she thought. *It has to be.* Her doctor had told her that the baby had probably become too big in her womb and had lain on his umbilical cord, cutting off his blood supply. *Maybe that's true, but that explanation does nothing for the guilt I'm feeling. I can't even have a baby. I can't do anything right.* The hardest part was when her two boys came to the hospital and asked, "Where's the baby, Mom?"

In the weeks following her child's death, Kim considered killing herself, but decided not to when she remembered that her husband and two children would be left behind. Still, she kept sinking further and further, until the day she suffered a nervous breakdown.

Kim was hospitalized, but at least she was able to receive some professional help. Doctors diagnosed her as a manic-depressive, a person who experiences incredible highs and incredible lows with not much in between.

Stuck in the hospital with time on her hands, Kim began listening to Zig Ziglar tapes again. One story from Zig seemed like it was meant for her.

"Zig elaborated on a story that he told in his book *See You at the Top,* in which he met a fellow named Bernie Lofchick in Kansas City, Missouri," said Kim. "It seems that Bernie introduced himself to Zig after a speaking engagement, and Bernie told Zig how his son, David, had overcome a tremendous battle with cerebral palsy to enjoy a fulfilled life.''

David was victorious because of the persistence, commitment, optimism and enthusiasm of his parents, Bernie and Elaine Lofchick. When the boy was very young, the parents visited thirty-one doctors before finding one they could believe and whose instructions they were committed to follow. It's been said that many people have gone a lot farther than they thought they could because someone else thought they could, and that's what happened with the Lofchick family. Bernie and Elaine believed in their child, and persisted in their belief by encouraging, pushing, prodding, but always loving. The results were astonishing. Today, at age forty, David is a happily married father of three, a healthy and successful businessperson with a bright future.

''Bernie and I hit it off,'' Zig said, ''because we had so many similarities. Both of us were from large families. Both of us lost our fathers at an early age. Both of us had worked in grocery stores as children. Both of us got into direct sales in the cookware business as very young men. Both of us overcame many difficulties, and as happens in rare instances, two men meet and a bond is formed.''

When they first met, Bernie's business was thriving and David was making considerable progress. Zig's career as a speaker was just beginning, and he was struggling. Bernie believed in Zig Ziglar as a speaker, and always labeled him as the ''greatest and most different motivator in all the lands.'' For this reason, Bernie often hired Zig to speak to his employees, and even helped Zig with financial assistance when the young speaker had trouble making ends meet. This was simply the way Bernie Lofchick did things. He makes people feel good, and if he believes in them, there is no limit to how far he will go with them.

One of Zig's fondest memories from those early, struggling days is when Bernie would take Zig to his tailor to have a couple of suits made for Zig while Bernie was having his own suits made. Bernie always laughed and said, "Brother Zig, if I wear the same suit you're wearing, people might mistake me for you, and nothing would make me more pleased!" This was more than just an act. That was the way Bernie Lofchick was. "He knew that I was struggling and couldn't afford the nice suits I really needed to make the right impression as a speaker," Zig remembers, "and that was his way of salvaging my pride while helping me in my professional career."

To this date, if you were to go into Bernie Lofchick's office in Winnipeg, Canada, you would see Zig Ziglar's name on the front of that office. Bernie laughingly tells people it really is Zig Ziglar's office, that Zig is only letting Bernie use it while he's there. What a guy!

The Lofchick family is extremely close. Bernie is proud of the fact that David has established a solid reputation as a businessman in his community, and when Bernie's youngest daughter, Mindy, graduated from law school, she was chosen out of two hundred applicants to be a Crown prosecutor, and gave distinguished service until she went into private practice. Myra, his other daughter, is living happily in Israel.

When you put it all together, to hear Zig talk about David and all the medical examinations, the thousands of hours of exercise and physical therapy, the hundreds of painful trips to the doctors and the therapists, how he learned to stand up on the frozen ice, the summers in the swimming pool, the weights he lifted as he strove to overcome his disease, it all ties directly into the rest of his family. Bernie displayed the same persistence in knocking on all of those doors selling cookware, in building his organization, and in influencing so many other people.

Since that time, Bernie has lost his mother, his sister and an older brother. As well, his beloved wife, Elaine, suffers from arthritis and spends most winters in Fort Lauderdale, Florida, but through it all that cheerful, upbeat attitude of encouragement is always present. Zig Ziglar says he has acquired much of his enthusiasm and optimism from Bernie.

"That's one of the neat things about motivation," says Kim. "Zig and Bernie inspired each other, and as I listened to Zig's tapes I, in turn, was inspired to continue in my struggle. In the process I learned to help and benefit other people."

Stories such as this one gave Kim purpose. In her mind, she now saw herself as:

1. A wife and parent who needed to persevere on behalf of her family.
2. A person who must be willing to receive help when it was freely given. For Kim, that meant seeking counseling for her manic depression.

Yet each time she listened to Zig and felt as if she were taking two steps forward in life, Kim took a big step backwards.

For instance, after the death of her child and her nervous breakdown, Kim sought solace in shopping, buying clothes, purchasing things she could not afford.

One time, when her oldest son had been hospitalized

for his asthma, she took off and drove two hundred miles from her hometown of Moscow, Kansas, to Wichita on a shopping spree. She maxed out her credit cards. "I had been at the hospital all day, and I was tired and so down," said Kim. "Then I thought, *I know what will make me feel better.* So I went shopping. That was my escape."

It wasn't long before the Whithams had to declare bankruptcy.

It was then that Kim needed to turn her life around *again.* Yes, she had listened to Zig Ziglar tapes before, but there was an important element missing—one that Zig often alluded to or spoke about directly.

It was the need for Christ. Kim heard Zig describe stories out of the Bible, and so she began reading the family Bible again. "After listening to Zig over and over, I just knew I had to get back to God," said Kim. "I had to quit asking why and just get back to Him."

At first, however, she was angry at God. Why did He give her a husband with the terrible Crohn's disease? Why did He give her such a sick first child? Why did He take her baby? Why did He let her spend the family into bankruptcy?

She sought solace, and she received it. The Scriptures reminded her to rest on the sovereignty of God, that He is in control and "that in all things God works for the good of those who love him, who have been called according to his purpose" (Romans 8:28).

Kim turned back to God and pleaded with Him to help her, and then she asked Jesus to take her guilt because she couldn't handle it anymore.

Kim turned a corner that day. She realized that she was not responsible for that snake biting her brother. She hadn't killed her baby, and the tiny child was in heaven.

She didn't need to charge up her credit cards to feel happy.

As Kim began to take a new look at life, she had the urge to share these revelations with others. Kim started talking with mothers grieving over the loss of their still-borns. Several Vietnam veterans in her small town had been struggling, so she offered to talk with them. "I share Zig, asking the vets to take a listen. His tapes have helped a bunch of them. At least that's what they've told me."

Sometimes, her newfound friends ask her what the biggest thing was she learned from Zig Ziglar.

"That's easy," she says. "It's being able to go back to God."

And the biggest gift Zig gave her?

"Getting myself and my family back."

Trent Gaites *

In the Futures Market

I grew up on the family farm hearing the following statement time after time from my parents: "Failure is an event, not a person."

That saying became a familiar refrain around my household. I struggled in school and received enough F's to start my own "F Troop." A failing mark was nothing to be proud of, however, nor was it something to broadcast to the world. I knew not to approach my grandmother and say, "Look, Grandma, I failed math this quarter." No, it was better not to say anything when failure struck. You hid the news.

I was taught to hold my head high and carry on, an attitude that carried Mom and Dad through the highs and lows of rural life in the deep South. Our family was poor but we were good country people. We never had anyone in our family go past high school until my older brother attended university, which prompted me to think about following in his footsteps. My mother recognized that I

*Due to the sensitive nature of this story, the family's names have been changed.

wasn't the brightest student in my class, however. She would always say, "God has given you other gifts," as if I was supposed to pick up the hint.

During my senior year of high school, my parents sat down with a guidance counselor on career night. "Mr. and Mrs. Gaites," the counselor began, "I do not believe that college is an option for Trent. This means I would recommend trade school."

When my parents relayed the conversation to me, Dad didn't say much, but Mom sensed I was crushed. She wrapped her arms around my shoulders and whispered, "If you wear a clean shirt and keep your shoes shined, you can go anywhere in life you want to go." I believed her. She said I had a way with people, and I could use that gift somehow. I could be a success in whatever I chose to do.

I refused to enroll in trade school. With her love and affirmation ringing in my ears, I was bound and determined to try higher education. I started at a local junior college, and later transferred to a university in Florida, but college life was not a breeze. My parents never heard the words "academic honor roll" and my name mentioned in the same breath. Still, I hung in there and squeaked by until I dropped out my senior year to enlist in the Marine Corps Reserves because I did not want to be drafted by the U.S. Army. There was a little thing called the Vietnam War going on.

After my active duty stint was over, I gravitated to the commercial cattle feed industry because of my love for cattle. After several years of long hours and hard work, I decided to step out and enter the commodity broker business.

Friends cautioned me, however, to keep my eyes wide open. They said the average broker lasts three years before he burns out or loses belief in himself. "You are going to get a lot of no's," said one broker friend. "It's not going to be easy."

"Well, if it was easy, they'd have Girl Scouts taking orders," I quipped.

"You'll see," counseled my friend.

I hustled and became one of the best commodity brokers in the South. One afternoon, a client took me aside.

"You want to know something?" he asked.

"What would that be?" I replied.

"The secret to this business is not making money. Making money is pretty easy. The secret is learning how to hold on to it and making it grow."

"That's right kind of you," I said, tipping my hat.

Making the right investment, I later learned, was going to be a major challenge.

CAUGHT UP IN THE MARKET WORLD

I became an overnight success in the commodities brokerage industry, specializing in cattle futures. In 1979, I was thirty years old, a devoted husband and father, ready for even more success.

While out prospecting one day, I made a presentation to potential clients who were in the midst of a start-up cattle-feeding operation. I must have made a great presentation because they asked me to throw in my hat with them. I knew how much money it took to feed cattle and keep that business going, but then again I had seen their corporate jet parked at a nearby airfield. It didn't take them long to convince me that this was a terrific ground-floor opportunity.

I invested our entire life savings and even borrowed

from my in-laws to help bankroll the new operation. Then I heard on the news that the Russians had invaded Afghanistan. I didn't think much of it until President Carter announced that he was suspending grain sales to the Soviet Union. This decision caused too much grain to flood the U.S. market, sending agricultural prices into a tailspin. When grain prices tumbled, the cattle market died.

The corporate jet was repossessed. The main financial backer disappeared. Creditors hounded the office.

I knew what all the events portended. When I told my wife, Mary, what had happened, she asked, "What are we going to do?"

"When the last of the cattle are sold and the business closes, we're going to have to go down to the bank and pay off our loans," I said.

She nodded, and although I could tell she didn't understand, I didn't want her to worry until the day of reckoning. Besides, her parents had put money into this cattle venture as well, and there was no need to roil the waters.

I made an appointment at the bank, and Mary and I walked in with my briefcase. The young man behind the desk must have been new because he was unaware of what was happening. He greeted us warmly and was all smiles as he started punching numbers into his machine, trying to figure out what the final payoff would be. A puzzled look came over his face. He started figuring again. After about ten minutes working the numbers, he turned to us and announced, "You've lost money."

"No kidding," I said.

Mary was more sanguine. "What do you mean, we've lost money?"

"Ma'am, you haven't lost money. You've lost a *lot* of money."

And there you have it. We lost practically everything we owned, including our house and our second car.

Driving home, Mary asked, "What are we going to do?"

"We're going to stay with my parents until we can get back on our feet again. I'm going to go back out there and get a job. We'll survive somehow."

I put our furniture in storage and packed up the car. As promised, I found another job in the brokerage industry because that line of work was all I knew. I had always been successful in the futures market, liked the business, and figured this was my family's best chance to recoup the horrific losses I had inflicted on them.

One day, while on a sales call, I ran into a gentleman in the cattle feeding industry who had heard about my plight.

"Son, I know what you're going through, and I think you need to listen to these," he said, handing me several audiocassettes of Zig Ziglar.

I had been exposed to some motivational speakers early in my career, and I found that sort of thing inspiring. In the cattle industry, you spend a lot of time driving from ranch to ranch, and I found it convenient to slip in one Zig Ziglar tape after another. Zig's message to me was: "So what if you've lost it? You'll gain it back." I believed him because of what he had experienced at forty-five years of age in losing it all before gaining it back again.

My favorite Zig principle became "You can have everything in life you want if you will just help enough other people get what they want." I know that quote is true because in helping other people, I've seen them want to help me in return. Zig had a way of taking things I already knew and saying them in ways that I could digest easily. Many of the principles that Zig promotes are Christian-based, but while I may have heard them growing up, they were never said in such an understandable way.

SPEAKING UP

As soon as I accepted a job in the brokerage business, I enrolled in night school and finished my last year of college. I was never a fast reader before, but for some reason, reading suddenly clicked with me, and I started to see the value in books. I read more and more. I credit Zig with this because he reminded me that it was never too late to learn.

Nor was it too late to pursue my dreams, and one of them was to become a speaker. For years in the brokerage business, I had been speaking in front of groups and had developed a little "dog and pony show" to make my presentations interesting and compelling.

The feedback I received after my talks jazzed me.

"I really like to hear you talk."

"We can really understand you. Keep it up."

"You speak really well. Have you ever thought about speaking full-time?"

In 1988, I left the commodity brokerage business to join a company selling information systems to rural America. My job was to train people to sell this technology in the Texas, Oklahoma and New Mexico markets. One time, I was attending a Young Farmers of Texas convention in Corpus Christi, where several hundred people waited for the company's director of education to address them.

Just a few minutes before he was scheduled to go on, the director said to me, "Listen, I'm a Yankee and they aren't going to listen to me. They will listen to you, however. You go and speak.''

Without any preparation, I stood up in front of the Young Farmers, and had a ball. When I finished, our booth was jammed for the remainder of the day, and I was suddenly inundated with speaking requests, from Amarillo to the Rio Grande Valley.

I thought all the attention was great. I began seeing myself as a junior Zig Ziglar. Although I had never seen Zig speak, I could imagine myself walking across that stage and taking that audience into the palm of my hand, just as Zig always does.

That incident ignited my speaking career, which started a little more than a decade ago. These days, whenever I travel to speak, I take one of Zig's cassettes with me. He has an energy that jumps out of that tape, which gives *me* energy. I've learned that the audience is only going to be as excited as you are.

I've needed that boost from Zig in recent years. In 1996, my oldest son, Rupert, was in the wrong place at the wrong time and got caught up in a situation in which he was charged with murdering someone in a bar. After he was arrested, Mary and I were introduced to the criminal justice system, which is a cruel lesson for any parent to go through. I took all the money that I had put away and wrote a check for a defense attorney—a high-priced one at that. My biggest concern, however, became Mary. She had been devastated, as you can imagine any mother would be.

Rupert was arrested in late August 1996 and not charged until December. Meanwhile, he languished in jail all fall. My attorney, who said I could be put on the stand

and have to testify against my son, would not allow me to talk to Rupert about the case. He was a good kid, my oldest child, an honor student all the way through school, but something must have happened that summer of 1996 to put him in the predicament.

This was a time for me to get back into those Zig Ziglar tapes. At a time when I felt the lowest, I needed to listen to something motivational. Since I was a self-employed speaker, I was trying to make calls on people and promote my business. I needed something that gave me a little lift so I could get through the day.

Just before the case went to trial, my son's attorney recommended a plea bargain, which the judge accepted. Rupert is now locked up in a maximum security prison serving a sixty-year sentence. He will be eligible for parole in thirty years.

After his sentencing, I looked my son in the eyes. "Life is a series of choices," I began, "and you've made some bad choices. I have, too. You are going to a place that you have no experience in. I know one thing for sure. There's a high road in there and there is a low road. The low road is crowded with people on it. You can get in there and wallow in the dirt and scum, if you want to. That will be the easy route.

"But there's also the high road, and I can assure you that it won't be crowded. There's always room at the top."

I offered to get Rupert books, and one of the first ones I sent to him was *See You at the Top*. He devoured it, along with books by Og Mandino, Napoleon Hill and Denis Waitley. Over the next few months, I saw my son experience a remarkable transformation. He took the high road, which was quite a challenge in a maximum security prison. He has tutored other prisoners to earn their GED degrees and is planning to enroll in a university program. He is not wasting his life.

Rupert has become involved with Prison Fellowship Ministries, the Christian outreach to prisoners started by Watergate figure Chuck Colson. I'm pleased he has gone that way.

I will not kid you and say that life has not been very difficult for me and my family in recent years. But I shudder to think where I would be if I had not received wisdom from the Bible and from Zig Ziglar.

Pam Lontos

Don't Tell Her It's Impossible
Until After She's Done It

Pam Lontos sat down with this book's researcher, Marsha Mc-
Clelland, to talk about the effect that Zig Ziglar had on her life.
Here is a transcript of that interview:

Marsha McClelland: Can you start off by telling me a little
bit about what you do?

Pam Lontos: I'm a motivational speaker and sales trainer.
I speak to associations and groups, write
magazine articles, consult for companies,
and have authored a book.

Marsha: What's the name of the book?

Pam: It's called *Don't Tell Me It's Impossible Until I've Already*
Done It.

Marsha: That's a great title. What is the book about?

Pam: Basically, the first part of the book recounts my life
story, and the second half is how to set and visualize
your goals while staying positive.

Marsha: You said you write magazine articles. Where have your articles been published?

Pam: Lots of different magazines, such as *Selling Power* or *Entrepreneur*.

Marsha: How did you come to hear of Zig Ziglar?

Pam: To answer that question, I have to start at the beginning. My childhood was not a happy one. My mom and dad often fought over money, so when I was fifteen, I took a job selling shoes on commission. When I brought money in, my parents didn't fight. My other escape was school because the classroom was the one place that if I did well, my father said something nice to me.

Marsha: You mean your mother didn't praise you?

Pam: No, she never did. Even when I did well on a test, my mother would find something negative to say. Plus, my parents were so strict. In my senior year of high school, at the age of eighteen, I couldn't go next door to visit a friend without asking permission, or I'd get grounded. I couldn't date, I couldn't do anything.

I was shy. I couldn't talk to people because my mind went blank, and I didn't realize at the time that was because of my poor self-esteem. I thought, *You know, you were born with a blank mind, and that is the way you are. You weren't born good enough.*

Marsha: What happened after high school?

Pam: I wanted to get out of the house, and my parents wanted me to marry an older man from our church, so I was married at age nineteen to a thirty-year-old man. At first the marriage was okay because I stayed busy. I took care of my husband, helped put him through dental school, cooked, cleaned, taught fourth grade, and went to night school twice a week. On Saturdays I sold shoes, so I didn't have time to get depressed.

When I was in my mid-twenties, we adopted two children. I stayed home to care for them and suddenly I didn't have my mind on other things. I became an overweight, depressed housewife. I couldn't get out of bed, so I slept for eighteen hours a day.

I hit rock bottom. I knew I had to do something.

Marsha: So what did you do?

Pam: I saw an ad in the newspaper for a local health club advertising a free workout. I was forty pounds overweight, so I thought this would help me take off a few pounds. I joined the health club and started an exercise program.

While working out at the club, I saw the people who were selling memberships, and I said to myself, *That looks like fun. I ought to try that.* I asked the owner of the health club for a job.

Shortly after I started, the owner gave me a set of Zig Ziglar tapes to take home.

Marsha: What series was that? Do you remember?

Pam: Let's see, this was 1975, so it would have been *How to Stay Motivated*. I can remember to this day lying on my couch, still depressed with the state of my life, and listening to those tapes for the first time. And Zig

Ziglar said, "People say you pay the price for success. But you don't pay the price for success; you pay the price for failure. You enjoy the benefits of success."

I had been paying the price of failure all my life. That was stupid. So I *really* started listening to those tapes—sixteen times on one side before turning it over. I mean, I wore out that first set.

If Zig said "Write this down," I did it. If he said "Do this three times a day," I did it ten times a day. When I got up in the morning, I slipped in a tape while I dressed. When I hopped in my car, I punched a tape into the cassette player. I learned certain Zig-isms by heart, such as, "You are what you are and where you are because of what has gone into your mind, and you can change what you are and where you are by changing what goes into your mind."

I listened to the tapes so much that within three months I became the top salesperson at the health club. Other people started selling just from being around me. It was amazing how motivated I became and how I went from a listless life to having a tremendous amount of energy.

I began helping the owner of the health club with radio advertising, and when I discovered I enjoyed radio sales even more, I went into radio sales in 1978. I also got more tape series from Zig, such as his *Career Building Course* and the *Richer Life Course*. I played them in the car while I drove to sales calls, and I became the top radio salesperson. In one month, six of us sold $42,000 in ads, and I sold $36,000 of it.

All this for a Dallas station that ranked near the bottom in ratings. A few years later, the sales manager quit, and when I applied, I got the job, not knowing that no one else wanted the job. What did I do with my staff? I brought out my Ziglar tapes and had them listen while they drove to sales calls.

In one month, just one month, we more than doubled sales, to $100,000, and a year later we were doing $275,000 a month—a 500 percent increase for a station with poor ratings.

Marsha: What did your boss think of this?

Pam: He couldn't believe it. Nor could the corporate owners—Disney's Shamrock Broadcasting. They asked me to fly to the corporate headquarters in Los Angeles, where they made me vice president of sales for Disney's radio and television stations.

Marsha: Wasn't this a little unusual?

Pam: Sure, it was. I had been in radio for two-and-a-half years. I had gone from a depressed housewife to a VP at Disney without a broadcast degree or anything. People said it usually takes twenty years to do something like that, and now I was in charge of their whole sales division, flying to all of Disney's radio and TV properties, training their people and working with their managers.

In January 1981, my senior VP at Disney called and said, "The National Association of Broadcasters wants you to speak at their annual convention in Las Vegas on how you raised sales at all of our 'dog' stations. People want to know how you did it with such poor rating numbers."

"They want to me to speak?" I asked. I was so shy that I often spoke with a whisper at parties. Two months earlier at a sales seminar, I couldn't even stand up and say my name. I had to ask the person who brought me to make the introduction.

Marsha: So what did you do?

Pam: I had to speak, and I knew Zig Ziglar was the greatest speaker, so in my innocence, I called Zig's office and said I wanted to meet him. They said he didn't have the time. "A lot of people want to meet him," I was told. But I learned that he was in his office on Mondays, but that was the only day, and he would be busy with all the work he needed to get done.

I had nothing to lose, so I drove over to his Dallas office and sat in his reception area all day. In the afternoon, his assistant, Laurie Magers, stepped out. I figured I had one shot.

"Zig says you can have everything in life you want by helping enough other people get what they want. I want to meet him. Go tell him that."

After she did, she said, "Mr. Ziglar will see you now."

I figured I had one minute to talk to him, so as fast as I could, I said, "Zig, I was an overweight, depressed housewife, sleeping eighteen hours a day, so I went and lost weight at a health club. I started selling memberships at the club, and they gave me these tapes of you. I listened to them, became the top salesperson at a radio station, and when they made me manager, we raised sales by 500 percent. I was promoted to VP at Disney, and now I've got to speak to the National Association of Broadcasters in Vegas, and I don't know how to give a speech. It's all your fault because if I hadn't listened to your tapes six years ago, I wouldn't have to do this speech now. So what am I going to do?"

He looked at me and said, "Miss Pam, I knew those tapes worked, but I didn't know they worked *that* good." And we shared a good laugh.

I was so in awe of him. I was getting to talk to Zig Ziglar! So he sat me down and gave me some tips: Talk to one person at a time. Make eye contact with that one person, and after four or five seconds, go to another person. Visualize yourself getting a standing ovation when it's all over.

When I went out to Las Vegas for the NAB convention, I thought I was going to be speaking in a small seminar room before thirty people. When they escorted me to two double doors and swung them open, I saw a huge ballroom with 2,500 people, a standing-room-only crowd. *Wait a minute, I thought. What happened to the small seminar?*

As I walked through the room, I introduced myself to various people. "Hi, I'm Pam. I'm going to be speaking. What do you do?"

"I'm president of ABC," one man replied.

Oh, no! What could I say to impress him?

When it was my turn to speak, I related stories about all the things I had learned from listening to Zig's tapes. I made eye contact. Spoke from the heart. When I finished, I received a standing ovation.

With the applause ringing in my years, someone from the Radio Advertising Bureau jumped on stage and said, "We want to put you on an eighteen-city tour."

"But what about Disney?"

"While you were speaking, they approved the idea."

Marsha: Did you do the speaking tour?

Pam: Yes, and things went so well that within a year I started my own company, Lontos Sales and Motivation. My friendship with Zig and Jean Ziglar deepened. He's been not only a great mentor, but Zig's also been a great friend, especially during my divorce. Several years later, in 1986, I told Zig that I was planning to marry Rick Dudnick, and he asked me to bring him over to his house so he and Jean could meet him. Rick got Zig's stamp of approval.

Marsha: Was there something in the tapes that you learned about relationships?

Pam: Yes. Be around positive people. I finally ended up with a good marriage because I have a mate who's positive and loving.

Marsha: If you had to define a "turning point" in your life, what was it?

Pam: It was when I first started listening to the Ziglar tapes on the couch that afternoon. I decided to be happy instead of being miserable. The action always comes first. If you're reading this book, you have to take the first step, and you do that by purchasing the Ziglar tapes. You have to pick up the Ziglar tape and put it in the cassette deck. Then you have to hear him speak in person. All these actions have to come before you can change what's going into your mind.

Someone once asked me, "How do you stay motivated?"

"Listen to the Ziglar tapes," I replied. "Listen to the tapes when you're driving in your car every day."

Marsha: What would you say is the greatest thing you have learned from Zig Ziglar?

Pam: That you are what you are and where you are because of what has gone into your mind, and you change what you are and where you are by changing what goes into your mind.

Marsha: Where do you think you'd be today if you'd never heard Zig Ziglar's tapes?

Pam: Dead.

Marsha: Seriously?

Pam: I probably would have committed suicide.

Marsha: Why do you say that?

Pam: Because of where I was headed. I didn't know I had a choice to be happy, successful and helping other people. I never knew I had a choice until Zig Ziglar came into my life and showed me.

Carolyn Ward

A Mary Kay-Meets-Zig Ziglar
Success Story

My parents, Emile and Anna Mae Rome, grew up in the maw of the Great Depression. Dad's father was a Mississippi riverboat captain who struggled to feed his nine children, while Mom was one of thirteen children growing up in the farming community of Opalousas, Louisiana. Like many who came of age in that era, Mom and Dad knew poverty firsthand. When they married for better or worse, they were determined to make a better life for themselves.

My father was a self-made man who put himself through Tulane University and earned an engineering degree. He worked for the U.S. Corps of Engineers in New Orleans just before I was born in 1939. Dad was an outgoing, very up kind of person who loved life and savored every moment. When a sales position with Raytheon Manufacturing Co. became available in San Francisco right after World War II ended, Dad grabbed the offer. "California, here we come!" he announced with glee one afternoon.

I was an only child, five years old at the time, when we moved to Burlingame, a half-hour drive south of his 49

California Street office in downtown San Francisco. My father said the Golden State was the place to be after the war—westward ho and all that. He wanted to expand our horizons, and that's where we spent the next eleven years.

My dad specialized in marine electronic sales for Raytheon, and he did well because he was dedicated and success-oriented. I can remember my father talking about large dreams and constantly repeating little sayings like "Where there's a will, there's a way," which meant I could do anything I wanted if I wanted it badly enough. Many years later, I was at Disneyland, and I saw a poster of an ant pulling an elephant up a hill with the caption, "Where there's a will, there's a way." I purchased it, and the framed poster sits in my office today.

I saw my father accomplish anything he wanted to do. He was a fine cook, proficient auto mechanic and self-taught musician who taught himself to play the banjo, piano and organ. He also tried to teach me that I was responsible for my own actions. "There's no such thing as a free lunch," he'd say, reminding me that I had to work for what I wanted.

We moved back to New Orleans in 1956 when my father was promoted to division manager for Raytheon. I finished my last year of high school and started college at Southwestern University in Lafayette, Louisiana, but quit after two years when I got bored. What I didn't know about myself at the time was that I am stimulated by people—not academics. I wish I had known that at the time.

WEDDING BELLS

After quitting college, I bounced through a series of dead-end secretarial jobs until I met a handsome second lieutenant in the Air Force named Larry Ward. We married in the fall of 1960 and were immediately transferred two thousand miles from home, to Glasgow, Montana. What a way to start a marriage, but I learned the value of commitment. When Larry and I had problems, I couldn't run home to Mom and Dad; we had to solve them ourselves.

Larry was a B-52 electronic warfare officer in the Strategic Air Command—SAC. Remember, this was the early 1960s, when the U.S. and Russia were rattling sabers during the height of the Cold War. Larry's job was defending nuclear-tipped B-52s from surface-to-air missiles over enemy territory should the unthinkable happen.

Since Larry was gone one week and then home one week, I had to learn to live alone on the base. I saw many Air Force wives pull up stakes and leave, but then I would hear my dad's voice: "You make your bed, and then you lie in it."

So I made friends. I learned how to play bridge. I enjoyed interesting small talk at coffee klatches. I asked for advice on how to raise Scott, our first son, after he was born in 1962.

Then the Air Force transferred us to Dyess AFB in Abilene, Texas, shortly before our second child, Kelly, was born in 1965. Larry was still flying B-52s for SAC, on alert.

Meanwhile, I was a young housewife who enjoyed being a mother, but at the same time, I knew that there was more between my ears than hair on my head. In 1966, there were few opportunities for women—especially mothers of small children. Office work was stifling, and besides, I wanted to be home with my two children as much as possible. I thought about selling Avon cosmetics, but door-to-door sales didn't appeal to me.

Then I received a knock on my door. Standing there

was my next-door neighbor saying that her cousin was visiting from Lubbock, and that afternoon she would be demonstrating a new line of cosmetics called Mary Kay.

"Would you like to come?" she asked.

"Oh, I don't think so," I said, more out of reflex than anything else.

"Why don't you come and get out of the house?" my neighbor persisted. "You don't have to buy anything."

I went, and of course, I purchased the five-step basic skin care package.

But another thing happened. At the end of the evening, the Mary Kay consultant came over to me and put her hand on my shoulder.

"Carolyn, you would be great doing this," she said.

"No not me," I demurred. "I couldn't sell a thing."

"Well, I think you could. Why don't you think about it?"

I went home and showed my new purchases to Larry. His first question was how much everything cost.

"Only $15.95, honey," which, in 1967, was still a tidy sum of money.

"You know what P. T. Barnum once said, don't you?"

"No, what was that?"

"He said there's a sucker born every minute, and I think you're one of them."

I thought to myself, *Ho, ho, buddy. You're going to eat those words. I'll prove to you that this stuff works.*

And three or four weeks later, Larry looked at me and admitted, "You know, I think that stuff is working. You told me that woman said you should consider selling it. Have you thought about that? I've heard you telling your friends about your Mary Kay products, and maybe selling them would be a good way to bring in extra money."

"But I don't think I could sell a thing," I responded. I was afraid of failing.

"Honey, I know you," said Larry. "You can do anything you make your mind up to do. I've seen you. I know you can do it."

Late that night I sat straight up in bed, in the dark, and thought, *My gosh, I think he's right. I can do this.*

The next day I looked in the Yellow Pages for a Mary Kay consultant, and a director named Stella Nowlin answered my call. I made an excuse that I wanted to pick up a lotion, but I really wanted to talk to her about how to get started selling Mary Kay. When I arrived at her house, I was greeted by this wonderful, warm person. I was immediately drawn to Stella.

I asked her to tell me more about Mary Kay Cosmetics. She outlined the story of Mary Kay Ash, who, in the early 1960s, was working for Stanley Home products, where she trained people. What Mary Kay noticed was that the glass ceiling was right above her head: Whenever an executive position opened in the company, the job went to a man— usually one she had trained!

A few years earlier, Mary Kay had become acquainted with a hide tanner who had discovered a process in which certain formulas softened the toughest skin. He thought if old animal skin could be softened with this process, why couldn't it work with human skin?

The hide tanner developed a five-step skin care formula, and when he passed away, Mary Kay purchased the rights to the formula and founded Mary Kay Cosmetics. She began selling in the Dallas area in 1963. Her company would be different: It would be *for* women because she believed women were capable of *anything* and, given the right opportunity, would excel in sales.

When I was introduced to Mary Kay, the company was just three years old. As Stella and I talked into the night, my heart was hammering. For the first time, I had a glimmer of hope that I could succeed through my own efforts.

I signed up immediately, and I was so determined that I told Larry, "I'm going to see this through if it kills me." The sales came quickly around Dyess AFB, and I found out I *could* sell, that I was a real people person and that I loved making money.

In fact, after five months as a consultant, I was doing so well that my husband and I talked about him getting out of the Air Force and moving the family back to New Orleans so we could be close to my parents. The stress of being in SAC was hard on Larry and the family.

We decided to take the plunge. Larry retired, and we moved to New Orleans, virgin territory for Mary Kay in those days, a place where I didn't have any customers.

Talk about hustle. I sold products and talked up Mary Kay as much as I could, since I was the family breadwinner while Larry looked for work. Then I attended the annual Mary Kay seminar in Dallas, which was held in a big auditorium. I saw women called up on stage and handed big commission checks, all to our applause.

I left Dallas a changed person, determined to become a director. Three months later, I went into qualification for directorship, which was based on production and the number of new consultants I brought into the company. I had to prove to the Dallas headquarters that I could do it. On April 1, 1968, I became a director.

The following year, I was attending one of my monthly Mary Kay director meetings in Dallas. There were less than one hundred directors back then (today, there are more than 8,000 directors and 400,000 consultants).

At our directors' meeting, Mary Kay Ash stood in a large conference room and said, "I've invited a guest speaker today, and his name is Zig Ziglar."

Zig Ziglar?

"I know Zig," she continued, "and I can assure you that he is one of the best motivational speakers I've ever heard. I think you'll agree after you've heard him today."

Remember the setting: This was 1969, and Zig Ziglar was just starting his full-time speaking career, mainly speaking in the Dallas area. But from the first minute, he took my breath away. I had never seen or heard anyone like him.

"Ladies, your attitude is more important than your aptitude," he began, and then he explained how he had heard about a Harvard University study showing that 85 percent of the reasons for success came from our attitudes and only 15 percent came from our technical expertise. "And let me tell you another thing," said Zig. "William James, the father of American psychology, stated that the most important discovery of our time is that we can alter our lives by altering our attitudes."

Zig described the difference between a pessimist and an optimist. "A pessimist says, 'I'll believe it when I see it,' and an optimist says, 'I'll see it when I believe it.' The person who is doing his or her best and is making a contribution is optimistic and confident because he or she is personally working on the solution. You, ladies, are working on the solution when you're working for Mary Kay."

Zig, who was in his early forties back then, had black hair and black horn-rimmed glasses. He was a slight, tall man who bounded all over the front of that room. The energy that man exuded was unbelievable, and he ignited every woman in that conference room during his one-hour talk.

Zig was also a pioneer in those days. He didn't mind talking to an all-female audience, no siree. Mary Kay consultants and directors from all over the country flew into Dallas for meetings, where they heard Zig Ziglar, and they returned to their hometowns talking about this amazing speaker. I'm sure Mary Kay was one of the reasons why Zig started to gain a national reputation.

When Zig finished speaking that day, he announced that he was available for workshops. Well, I wanted some of that action. I asked him to come to New Orleans to talk to my consultants. He told me his fee was $5 per head, but he would pay his expenses.

I picked him up at the airport, and back then it was just Zig—no sound crew, no entourage. He spoke that evening to fifty of my consultants in a Howard Johnson's meeting room, receiving only $250. But this was pure Zig, circa 1969.

I can see him now, impacting those consultants as he did in Dallas. He was awesome, and I knew their lives would never be the same. He was the first motivational speaker that I ever brought in, and he returned in 1971.

In the years to follow, Zig became the household name that he is today. In fact, I remember one time—it must have been the early 1980s—when I was in a meeting with Mary Kay Ash. We were discussing bringing in a guest keynote speaker for the annual Mary Kay seminar.

"Hey, why don't we bring Zig back!" said one national sales director.

"Honey," replied Mary Kay, "I don't think we can afford him now."

We all laughed at the irony in the statement, but everyone at Mary Kay is happy that Zig has reached the zenith of the motivational speaker industry.

Zig's teachings have had a huge impact on my life. I have risen to the position of executive senior national sales director and have earned my way into Mary Kay's inner circle. To be a member of the inner circle, you must have earnings of over $300,000 a year. My primary responsibility is to train and motivate directors at the management level while impacting consultants in the sales force to move up to management.

Looking back, I see that Zig Ziglar has been a huge thought-changer in my life. Even though I grew up with positive and upbeat parents, Zig put into words why I had to stay positive and not put a limit on my thinking.

For me, Zig came along at the right time, in 1969. I was privileged to be exposed to Zig before he became "Zig Ziglar," but there is one thing that remains the same— Zig's humility. Having seen and heard him for over thirty years, I can assure you that he is as humble now as he was back then.

Christopher Doyle

The Karate Kid

The world record attempt was six months in the planning. Eight-foot tables had to be rented, cinder blocks procured, and six hundred wooden boards—all 1×1s one foot long—purchased.

Christopher Doyle, a black belt in karate, was poised to smash the world record for "board breaking" by hand-chopping six hundred boards in one minute. For him to successfully crack a half dozen boards with each blow, he and a band of volunteers would have to set the boards with military precision so precious nanoseconds could be saved.

News stations and newspapers in Christopher's hometown of Toronto, Canada, were notified of the world record attempt. On the big day, more than 120 volunteers toiled eight hours to set up each table and all the boards just so. No detail was too insignificant.

Christopher had once busted ninety-six boards in sixty seconds, but that was just a warm-up. Now he was shooting for 600 in 60—his new mantra—a feat that could put him in the *Guinness Book of World Records*.

That's quite a goal, Christopher said to himself when he began training for the world record attempt. Fortunately,

Christopher had been listening to Zig Ziglar for nearly ten years, and learning to set goals had become as natural as breathing for the thirty-two-year-old Canadian.

But the first time Christopher heard Zig Ziglar, his message had hit him like a karate kick.

A CANADIAN IMMIGRANT

Christopher Doyle was born in England, but he and his family emigrated to Canada when he was five years old. The family moved in with relatives, and young Christopher remembers being ruthlessly teased by an uncle—only sixteen years of age—about not having a place to live. The Doyle family eventually moved into a cramped two-bedroom flat.

Christopher was born with a blistering temper; relatives blamed the "fighting Irish" blood coursing through his veins. Suffering from low self-esteem and picked on by playmates, Christopher learned to talk with his fists, frequently lashing out at others. On more than one occasion he was suspended from school for using his dukes.

A childhood movie affected his psyche. Called *Cipher in the Snow,* the film depicted a young child riding the bus to school. In the middle of the route, the boy gets up out of his seat and taps the school bus driver on the shoulder.

"I want to get off," he says.

The bus driver thinks that's kind of strange, especially in the dead of winter with tons of snow on the ground. But he complies, and he lets the boy off the bus.

The boy bounds down the steps, walks over to a snow pile, collapses and dies. A teacher is designated to find out why the boy wanted to die. A background check reveals that he was a good kid until his parents divorced. Two of the adult authorities in his life, however—his stepfather and teacher—went out of their way to belittle him, causing the child to feel like a big fat zero—a cipher.

That's how Christopher saw himself during much of his childhood, and to gain attention, he talked with his fists. His father didn't know what to do with his thirteen-year-old roughneck, so he placed him in a martial arts class. Thinking he would learn how to fight even better, Christopher immediately loved the sport, but he quickly learned that martial arts was not karate chops to the solar plexus or lightning-quick kicks to the groin.

Instead, martial arts is an icy discipline that places a premium on controlling your emotions and temperament, which was a revelation to Christopher. At the same time, he found the martial arts to be a friendly environment where devotees pushed themselves. "I was taught that I was the one in charge, and the person who is in charge will win. I could not give up until I won."

Such thinking lifted the self-esteem of the emigrant teenager, who embarked on a five-year goal to earn his black belt in karate. He became a formidable foe, filling out a six-foot frame with 195 rock-hard pounds by the time he entered the University of Guelph, ninety minutes west of Toronto. "The black belt is a commitment to defend yourself and all the ideas and principles of the black belt," Christopher explained. "That's what I wanted for myself."

As he continued to grow in stature and gain a reputation in karate circles, the owners of his studio recognized his natural-born leadership and offered to help him start his own martial arts studio.

"I'm a good talker, and I wanted to help people learn the martial arts, so I took their financial backing," said

Christopher. "They told me I could pay them back in the first year."

There was just one little problem: Christopher was still a full-time student at the University of Guelph. Ever since the family landed on Canadian shores, Christopher's father had informed him and his sister that one of the reasons they emigrated was to get good educations, and part and parcel was the assumption that the two children would attend and finish college.

Christopher had a dilemma. Bored by school, he looked around and saw other martial arts studio owners doing quite well throughout the Toronto area. He was ready to strike out on his own, so he made a choice to drop out of college and throw himself into his own martial arts studio.

Christopher had a great background in martial arts—but none in business. From early on, the studio did not click. He had trouble attracting students; it was a struggle to keep one hundred coming through the doors each week. The break-even point was two hundred students.

Month after month the Academy of Martial Arts lost money, and Christopher moved out of his apartment and started sleeping on a cot in his office. He cut down to eating one meal a day and lived off his credit cards.

Thoughts of becoming a business failure flooded his mind, and all those suppressed feelings of inferiority from his childhood rose up again. "I was supposed to be this big martial arts guy, but when the business went south, I always told my parents that I was too busy to see them, that I had to give a seminar or teach another class, instead of saying, 'I need help.' "

He managed to keep the doors open, but Christopher

knew if something about his life did not change soon, his dream business would one day be padlocked. One afternoon before the start of classes, he visited some downtown bookstores. He needed to find *something*. While perusing the racks at one bookstore, he stumbled across a Zig Ziglar audiocassette.

He was immediately drawn to the warm drawl of Zig's presentation, but one phrase hit him like a swift kick to the stomach: "You are what you are and where you are because of what goes into your mind," intoned Zig.

Really? You mean I have the power to impact the direction my life takes?

"I started doing the opposite of what I had been doing," said Christopher. "Instead of saying to myself, *I feel worthless . . . I can't make it . . . There are too many stresses to deal with . . .* , I started focusing on the opposite. I began saying to myself, *I feel happy, healthy, wealthy and wise, in charge and energized.* I can remember waking up in the middle of the night and thinking, *Happy, healthy, wealthy and wise, I'm in charge and energized.* It got to a point where it was a mantra. I was no longer drinking bad water; I was drinking fresh springwater."

When Zig talked about the struggles he experienced while selling pots and pans, Christopher thought, *There's somebody who knows what it's like to go through rough times.* Christopher had been putting the weight of the world on himself, and he needed help.

"In martial arts, the word *karate* means 'empty hand' and 'open mind,' " said Christopher. "I had forgotten what I do best, which is to open my hand and my mind and let things go. I had a closed mind and a closed spirit. I had been holding on to things too closely, trying to do everything by myself, when in reality I needed help."

Help came from his parents and others in the martial arts industry, and Christopher enlisted them in getting the studio back on its financial feet. Ever since then, he's never looked back.

A COMMITMENT TO COMMITMENT

There's another thing that Christopher learned from the Ziglar tapes: the meaning of commitment. When Christopher heard Zig describe the *real* meaning of the word, he knew Zig was speaking directly to him about his girlfriend, Lesa MacDonald. Then and there, he knew it was time to step up and marry Lesa. "After listening to Zig talk about the importance of commitment, I asked Lesa to marry me. A lot of men have trouble committing to something. The commitment to marriage taught me that if you are going to say you will do something, then do it."

Something interesting happened after his marriage: Christopher found it easier to commit to his students, his studio and his business. He spoke with more authority and more passion, and he inspired his students to push themselves. He asked them to reevaluate how they looked at ordinary events in their lives. Did they set their "alarm clocks" every night or their "opportunity clocks"? Were they setting *Smart* goals, as Zig suggested, ones that were *specific, motivating, achievable, rewardable* and *trackable?*

It didn't take long for word of mouth to hit the streets that the Academy of Martial Arts was the place to be, and Christopher's classes filled to overflowing. He became a well-known teacher in the Toronto area, and in 1998, he was invited to train for three weeks in Okinawa, the Japanese island that is known as the birthplace of karate. Based on his performance in Okinawa, Christopher was asked to return to the 1999 World Championships held on the island.

He has adapted Zig's positive outlook to the world of karate. "If I hold up a blank piece of paper with a black dot on it and ask, 'What does everyone see?' everyone looks at the paper and says, 'Hey, there's a black dot there.' In reality, there's more white space than the one black dot. Zig Ziglar taught me to focus more on the bigger picture—the white paper—than on the small dot in my life. And that's what I tell my students."

A WORLD RECORD ATTEMPT

The videocams were there, along with the print reporters and newspaper photographers. They were all awaiting the quest for "600 in 60," the world record in board breaking.

Christopher was in superb physical condition, probably the best shape he had ever been in. Dressed in his white *gi*, tied by a black *obi*, he concentrated and began breathing deeply, focusing his energies on the nearly insurmountable task at hand.

The countdown began. At the count of zero, Christopher became a whirlwind of chopping activity, and dozens of boards split in two with the passing seconds. Racing against the clock, he slammed his stiff right hand against the stacked 1×1s, breaking them in two with a flourish.

When the buzzer sounded, Christopher had smashed 495 boards in just sixty seconds—a new world record! Although he hadn't reached his goal of "600 in 60," he had obliterated the old world record by seventy-five boards— and raised $2,000 for Childfind Canada, a charitable organization.

Christopher's exploits became part of the national and international news cycle, and CNN broadcast a quick clip around the world. Christopher's father was at his father's funeral in Ireland, and he beamed with pride as he watched his son do what no man had done before.

There was one more person who had to know about the world record: Zig Ziglar. Christopher wrote a personal letter to his mentor, outlining the role he played.

Not long afterward, Christopher received a letter of congratulations from Zig.

"Now *that* was really neat," he said.

Gina Lopez*

The Prodigal Daughter

I remember my elementary school years like yesterday because the pain still runs deep. Classmates called me ugly and beat me up on the playground. Even my teachers picked on me; I remember one saying, "Do you think you could wash your face before you come to school?"

My face probably wasn't washed because I was raised by neglectful parents. They didn't scrub my face or remind me to brush my hair or show me how to dress. Kids picked up on that, and I went through school being pointed at and giggled about. Although I love my parents and I'm as close to them today as I've ever been, I grew up with a mother who drank herself into a stupor each afternoon. I would come home from school and find wine bottles littered everywhere and Mom passed out on the couch. ABC-TV could have done one of those *After School Specials* on our family.

Life got a little better in junior high when the kids tired of making fun of me and turned their attention to others who didn't quite fit the mold. Dad and Mom had

Due to the sensitive nature of this story, Gina Lopez is an alias.

enrolled me in a private school, where I wore a uniform each day. I was discovering boys and craving male attention, so once the uniform came off, I wore lots of makeup, low-cut shirts, short skirts, and high heels. I did that because it made me feel pretty and boosted the low self-image I held of myself. Maybe that's why I started shoplifting. I stole all my clothes, makeup, and perfume so I could be like everyone else.

There's no doubt I was a lost child, and my parents didn't know what to do with me. I was a mixed-up teen who was looking for love, and like the song says, I found it in all the wrong places. I sought sexual attention from guys, which gave me a little lift at the time, but in the long run giving up my body ruined what little self-esteem I had. I could barely read, and as I went through the school system, I don't think my teachers knew what to do with me. I never did a lick of homework in my life, and I was as wild as they came. When I turned eighteen, I graduated from high school with a report card full of Fs. I don't know why they even gave me a diploma.

After graduation, I hooked up with my friend Linda, who had just moved into an apartment along the Massachusetts coast. "I'm impressed," I told Linda as I surveyed her new digs and checked out the beach from her balcony. Her beautiful apartment was furnished with gorgeous furniture and outfitted with the best stereo equipment money could buy.

"Why don't you live with me?" she asked, and I quickly agreed.

There was always a party going on at Linda's apartment, with a lot of cool guys—mostly Dominicans—hanging out all the time. They seemed to have a lot of cocaine, and since it was being passed around for free, why not take a blow? I also began drinking heavily with them.

My newfound friends asked if I could do a favor for them. Could I fly from Boston to New York and bring back a couple of kilos of coke?

"It'll be easy, no sweat," they promised. "There's no customs to go through, and we'll even pack the coke in your boots so your fingerprints won't be on it."

I agreed and flew down to New York City and took a cab to the projects on the upper West Side, where I was to pick up the cocaine. I took the elevator to the twenty-second floor and entered an apartment where everyone had guns. I hung out and did coke with them, and for fun, they took me outside and showed me how to use an Uzi machine gun. These guys just loved their guns; they even slept with them.

I began to make frequent trips between New York and Boston each time carrying drugs. It was an exciting life and I loved spending time in New York. My new friends always had cocaine and always shared. If I spent more time with them, I began to hear cryptic conversations about people being killed, but I didn't want to listen too closely. One time, I came back to the apartment to discover that it had been ransacked and $22,000 in cash stolen from a safe. Things were getting really crazy, and I feared for my safety.

This was the lowest point of my life. I had moved into an apartment with my boyfriend, who was part of the Dominican gang, but in a matter of weeks he ditched me, leaving behind a ton of bills, including the lease on the furniture, long-distance phone calls, and unpaid stereo equipment. I had little choice but to declare bankruptcy. Not a great way to start your life when you are nineteen years old.

With no money and no options, I moved back in with Mom. I was very depressed, and it was all I could do to get myself out of bed in the mornings. One day, I was flipping channels on the TV when I came across a commercial selling Zig Ziglar's three tape series called "See You at the Top," "Goals" and "Self-Image." All of his series contained six to eight tapes each.

I was searching for something, but I was so messed up I didn't know what it was. What attracted me to the commercial was how the host keyed in on my need to make goals as a way of becoming "normal" again. I was tired of being different, tired of being an outcast.

I ordered the series and listened to Zig Ziglar's tapes every night. Over and over I let his message of hope and positive attitude sink in. I had been putting garbage into my life, and like Zig said, I had been reaping nothing but garbage as a result. I liked the idea of trying to grow flowers in my mind instead of all those weeds.

Zig's tapes also created an urgency to finally start doing *something* with my life. I was wasting it by hanging out with some very evil people. I was traveling in the fast lane, and if I didn't get off, I probably would become a stripper— or worse. But Zig changed the whole direction of my life.

Goals. You have to set goals, said Zig.

Let's see. I wanted an education. I wanted a nice apartment with nice furniture. I wanted to be successful and have a good life. I wanted to be debt-free.

Those were the big goals I wrote down. Then Zig asked me to create a "wild idea list" of things I wanted to accomplish in my life. I noted in my Ziglar planner that I wanted to waitress at T.G.I. Friday's restaurant, become a manicurist and work out regularly in a gym. You may not be impressed, but these were high goals for someone with a limited education who once got fired from one of the easiest jobs in the world—being a telephone operator.

After hearing Zig, I experienced a total transformation, just like those makeovers you see on TV. First, I worked on my outside. I enrolled in beauty school. I visited make-up counters at mall department stores. I asked hairstylists to try every hair color known to Lady Clairol. I hired the services of an image consultant. I attended a modeling school, where I learned to walk, talk, and eat well. I even had liposuction done on my body.

Then I learned through Zig that I had to work on something more important than my physical appearance: the inside of me. Although I had changed the way I looked, I still had behavior problems.

I needed immediate help with my drinking problem, so I entered Alcoholics Anonymous. I embarked on the twelve-step program, which gave me the motivation to stop pitying myself and take action. At Alcoholics Anonymous, I learned to change my behaviors. Of course, the number-one thing was stop the drugs and drinking, but there was more. I was a slob. I never made my bed. I never cleaned my bathroom. I didn't eat right, take vitamins, or keep a regular sleeping schedule.

It was about this time that I met Billy. I'm not sure what bonded us together, but he's intelligent and focused. He has goals. He wants to make something of his life. When he couldn't walk through my bedroom without tripping, he became exasperated with me. He bought me John Atwood's video on deep-cleaning your house and Jeff Campbell's video on speed-cleaning. These days, my place is always picked up and tidy so I can have company anytime.

Some of that company, however, may not have been the best type of folks, if you catch my drift. Billy also helped weed the wrong people out of my life. Instead of saying, "No, you can't hang out with so-and-so," he would say, "These people are not helping you. Can't you see that those people have problems?"

"No," I would reply. "What are you talking about?"

"You don't know? Well, let me explain a few things," and Billy would help me see the light.

Another important ingredient of my comeback was going back to school, not only did I return to college and earn an associate's degree, but I also participated in an eight-week "coaching" program put together by Zig Ziglar's organization. Each week for a half-hour, a Ziglar coach would call and ask me things like:

- How you are doing in your Performance Planner?

- How are you doing on your homework?

- Did you read another chapter of Zig's book, *Over the Top?*

The coaching program brought me to another level, which has energized me to set even more goals. I have this silly pipe dream of making a Movie of the Week out of my life, which would open with me hanging around the Dominican gang in New York City and then show how I went through my changes. The movie would fade to black with me meeting Zig Ziglar. That would be really cool! I haven't met Zig yet, but I want to meet him so badly. I really believe that God is using Zig as an angel in my life.

I'm really happy with the way my life is going. I'm the

number-one salesperson at a phone company, and with commissions, I'm bringing home a salary that I never dreamed could happen to me. I've been able to purchase my own town house with a Jacuzzi, and if things keep going well, I can have it paid off six years from now when I'll be thirty-seven years old.

I'm very proud of what I've accomplished in life, especially when I look back and see where I was and where I've gone. Not long ago, I wrote Zig a letter to thank him for being my mentor and for changing my life at a time when I could have gone either way. I could have become a druggie doing tricks, but with Zig's help, I chose to have the good life I'm enjoying now.

I received a letter back from Zig, and it's one that I reread and cherish every time I pull it out. Here's what it says:

Dear Gina:

I have to say that your letter is one of the most exciting I have ever received. Congratulations, Gina, for having what it takes to command control of your life and where it's going. I appreciate more than you can know you sharing so much of your story with me. I'm both encouraged and inspired to continue to share the message of setting and reaching goals to enjoy a balanced and satisfying life.

The goal setting and reaching instructions are usually the part of Over the Top *which most participants mention as being particularly helpful to them. The goal setting is such a critical function of overall life. I am pleased to know that you, too, feel that it has been bene-*

ficial. I am also pleased, but not surprised, that Sandy Bigelo has been an effective coach for you.

Keep up the good work, Gina. Have a good forever, and I will definitely See You Over the Top.

Zig Ziglar

Chris Leto

Looking Up All the Way

Growing up, Chris Leto was always the smallest player on his Little League baseball team. One time while batting, a fan good-naturedly yelled out, "Why don't you stand on a phone book?"

When Chris heard that, he thought it was the funniest thing he had ever heard. Then he pointed his bat at the fan and stepped back into the batter's box. On the next pitch, he rapped a game-winning double down the left field line.

On the field, Chris was a intense shortstop. Once, while turning a double play, Chris took the throw from the second baseman and pivoted to relay the ball to first base for the second out. The opposing player didn't slide into second base, and was thus blocking his throw to first base. The opposing player never believed Chris would make the throw if someone was in the way.

Chris had a split second to determine what he was going to do, and his instincts told him not to back down. So he whipped the throw to first base. Unfortunately for the runner, the ball drilled him in the middle of the chest. You can bet the runner never did *that* again.

"It was either him or me," recalled Chris, "and it wasn't going to be me."

Perhaps Chris gained this never-back-down attitude from his father, Sam, who was also his Little League coach. "He was a great manager," said Chris, "and he told me, 'I know you are never going to be six feet tall, but you have great talent. You've got a heart that's bigger than anyone's. Since you're my son, you're going to have to prove it more than anyone else.' "

All through adolescence, baseball was Chris Leto's life. He always played on winning clubs—all-star teams that went to national tournaments. One year, his team advanced to the World Series and came in second, losing to the favored team from Taiwan, 2–1 in fourteen innings. Chris went on to star in high school competition, but when he considered playing baseball in college, some people told him, "You're too small. You can't play."

"My attitude was *I'll show you!*" said Chris. *"I may be five-foot, four inches tall, but I'll fight you and I'll beat you."*

No wonder Chris was known as the "spark plug" of the team. "During my teenage years, I was confident, aggressive and had a winning attitude."

Too small to be recruited, Chris went off to a university in Southern Florida with designs on earning an engineering degree. He approached the baseball coach and asked for a tryout. "Walk-ons," as they were called, faced infinitesimal odds. But then the star shortstop got hurt. The next thing Chris knew he was playing against Division I college powerhouses such as Miami, Florida State and Texas.

Chris responded in his usual manner by playing above his head, and the seniors on the team took a shining to him. The head coach, however, didn't share the same feelings, and all season long Chris endured degrading remarks about his height and his Hispanic-Italian heritage. Furthermore, his class work was suffering.

After he'd had much discussion with his dad, who knew him better than anyone else, they sized up the situation and agreed that the best option was earning a college degree and coming to work in the family business. Regrets? "Absolutely," replied Chris. "This was the end of a dream, but it was the right decision."

Chris finished college with an mechanical engineering degree in hand and joined his father, mother and grandfather at the family-owned Tampa Brass & Aluminum Corporation, a foundry and machine shop that produced high-tech parts for missiles and mechanical components for major defense contractors and original equipment manufacturers. The company had been founded by Chris's grandfather and father in 1957.

His father and old baseball coach was the CEO, but this time they were teammates, and together they faced problems much bigger than bases loaded and nobody out. In the late eighties, Tampa Brass teeter-tottered between solvency and bankruptcy when a bank failed to come through with agreed-upon financing.

Meanwhile, Chris married the girl of his dreams, Joy Walters, who became his best friend and encourager. Soon after the nuptials, Joy became pregnant, but doctors called it a "high-risk" pregnancy. Their fears were proved correct when during the sixth month the unborn baby died in the womb. "I still have this picture ingrained in my head of when the baby boy was delivered stillborn," said Chris, "and this happened ten years ago."

Soon afterward, Tampa Brass was forced to file chapter 11 bankruptcy protection. "We did everything we could to work something out with the bank without having to file, but they refused to speak with us unless it was through the courts," Chris recounted. "To survive, we had to take serious pay cuts. Our pride was hurt. I was watching a family business that had flourished in the seventies and eighties be put in jeopardy of closing its doors. But we never quit. My dad somehow kept it going."

The biggest blow, however, came in 1992 when Chris and his family began to experience tremendous electrical problems in their machines. In the middle of a clear day, various machines would "alarm out" (stop working), indicating a short or unexplainable surge of power. These instances were burning up the computer boards and controls inside the $150,000-to-$300,000 machines.

For sixteen months, engineers, electrical experts and the power company monitored all the power, but they could not solve the mysterious occurrences. In February 1994, after a large explosion in the control panel room caused a fire that shut down the entire plant for a week, evidence of sabotage was discovered.

"I watched my mom faint right there when she was told the news," said Chris. "Over those sixteen months, the saboteur cost us over $400,000 in repair costs, not counting lost time, missed deliveries and angry customers. The evidence pointed to the involvement of an employee. When we confronted him, he vehemently denied everything, defending his friendship to us and saying he would never do anything to hurt the company. When we asked him to take a polygraph test, he turned belligerent, threatening my father.

"As Tampa Brass battled for survival, we cashed out all our insurance policies, borrowed from my grandmother's retirement plan and received loans from friends and relatives. In addition, I personally borrowed over $125,000 from more than fifteen credit cards to keep the company alive.

"We battled the insurance company, who thought it was dealing with a weak and unstable company that was not going to survive. At that point, they were probably right. The insurance company fought us every step of the way, using incredible tactics to avoid paying us for the damages.

"Finally, we won the jury trial in September 1995, proving the insurance company had been negligent as a carrier. The jury awarded us full damages of $1.2 million, plus interest. However, as our glorious judicial system would have it, a successor judge ordered a new trial based on a technicality. We currently have an appeal filed under the jurisdiction of the Florida Supreme Court. What a character-building process this has been!"

AN EXTRA TICKET

Times of trial teach lessons, and Chris was learning that the only things of any worth were his family (they have two sons now), his extended family and his friends.

"Everything else crumbled. It was horrible. I felt like I was a victim of terrible circumstances. My business was going to be lost, and there was nothing I could do about it."

This is where Chris's life made a turning point. Yes, it happened through Zig Ziglar. In 1994, a sister-in-law had an extra ticket for a Peter Lowe Success Seminar.

"I had no idea who Peter Lowe was," said Chris. "My sister-in-law said the all-day event was about being successful, and boy, did I need that. So I went."

At 8 A.M., the first speaker strode onto the stage. His name was Zig Ziglar. "Man, did he light up the crowd at that early hour, the first thing in the morning," remembered Chris.

"Do you think there's something you can do in your life to make it worse?" asked Zig.

"Yes," said Chris, along with nearly twenty thousand others at St. Petersburg's Thunderdome.

"Is there anything you can do that will make your life better?" asked Zig.

That question wasn't so easy to answer, but most replied yes enthusiastically. As those in attendance fidgeted, Zig said, "Then what you've said to me is that you can do whatever you want in life to make it better or worse. Am I right? Then the choice is yours."

The choice is mine? thought Chris.

Then Zig brought Christ into the equation. "Jesus Christ is the faith and power of everything," said Zig. "With prayer and with hope, you can do it."

Something spiritual, something deep, stirred within Chris's soul. Sure, he believed in God, but before he heard Zig Ziglar, he didn't really *know* God.

Besides, where had God been during his times of trial? Where was God when Chris felt anger, hurt, disappointment, fear and terror?

Chris bought Zig's *See You at the Top* at the Success Seminar and started reading it that night. "I probably read it five times over the next three months," said Chris. "I took what he said and wrote down the goals that I had, which were all mumbled and jumbled. It took me five or six months to get all my thoughts in order. Zig broke it down for me. He said make a plan for what you want to do. Then ask yourself these questions: Why do you want it? Who is going to benefit? Who will not benefit?

"Then Zig narrowed it down even further. For instance, if I wanted to sail around the world, why would that be important to me? Would it be more important to have all the money in the world or to have a wife and two kids that admire me as the greatest husband and father?"

Those questions prompted Chris to develop spiritual goals, charitable giving goals, personal goals, career goals and "toys & adventure" goals—fun goals. In his heart, Chris knew his biggest spiritual goal should be to get closer to God, so he started attending Sunday church services regularly. He later attended a Promise Keepers event and a men's church retreat that further inspired his faith. "Reading and listening to Scripture has increased my awareness, understanding and love for God and others," he said.

Since Chris became "Ziglarized," he has helped Tampa Brass & Aluminum get back on its feet and become strong in spite of not being reimbursed for over $1 million in damages. From Zig's lessons, he is inspiring other family members to stay focused and optimistic that the future will be even better. Younger brothers Tim and Jason work at Tampa Brass as a controller and production manager, respectively, while sister Julie is Chris's assistant in sales and marketing. His mom, Nilla, does all the purchasing.

Chris reports that most of his credit cards have been paid off and the company's customer base is growing. Sales have almost tripled since 1993. "During this time of trial, our values were never compromised," said Chris. "A year or so ago, I received my greatest compliment ever. My father, the CEO, told me that the business never would have made it if it wasn't for me. That's reassuring!"

As for his personal goals, Chris said that he's decided that "every day is going to be my greatest day. My first goal is to be able to inspire people to change their lives just like Zig inspired me to change mine, regardless of their circumstances. I want to be the best husband, father, son and friend and become proficient in CPR so that maybe one day I can save a life. I want to earn a third-degree black belt and work with the kids at the Boys and Girls Club, where I donate my time. At work, I want to grow Tampa Brass beyond existing horizons and eventually help people in America and in the world. I want to be ready to run the company when my sixty-year-young father retires."

SEE YOU AT THE COURTSHIP

There's another Ziglar book that Chris has read, called *Courtship After Marriage,* which is also the name of a tape series by Zig. Chris read it not because his marriage was experiencing problems, but because he wanted to make a great marriage even greater.

The biggest thing he learned was that he was forgetting to express appreciation to Joy. Zig wrote:

> *When your mate does anything that makes your trip through life a little easier, a sincere thank-you is important and appreciated. If you expect your mate to do something because it's his or her "job" or responsibility, the odds are long that it will be done reluctantly, poorly or not at all. If you express appreciation, results are far better. And you want to know something? Those little thank-yous are indications of class. Perhaps you remember your mother's admonishment that we might not all be rich and smart, but we can all be kind and courteous and do little things for each other every day. If husbands and wives will do something every day for each other that their mate*

is perfectly capable of doing, it's amazing how that will enhance the romance in their marriage.

My wife has been recognized as one of the better car-door-openers in the Dallas metropolitan area, but in all our years of marriage she hasn't opened her car door more than a dozen times when I was with her. One of my delights has been to walk around and open her door for her because it's a clear reminder that my wife is the most important person in the world to me. She is one to whom I have committed my life, and the only woman I have ever loved.

Many years ago, I stopped carrying money in my wallet and began to simply fold it over and keep it in my pocket. At night I lay my cash on the bathroom counter. Soon after I realized the Redhead (as I lovingly refer to her, although I call her "Sugar Baby" when I'm talking to her) counted the money, and if she thought I didn't have enough to cover any emergencies when I was going out of town, she would go to the bank or store and get some more cash for me. That's not a big deal, but what it said to me was, "Honey, I feel more comfortable knowing that if there are emergency situations where you need a little extra cash, you won't be embarrassed or endangered for lack of it." Like I say, it's no "biggie," but actions like those speak volumes to me.

For the first time, Chris began to see that it was the little things he could do for Joy that could make big differences in their marriage. Today, Chris not only opens the car door for Joy, but when they are in a restaurant, he always rises out of his chair when she arrives and when she leaves the table. He also always pulls away her chair when she's ready to sit down. Then he listens to his friends' wives says to their husbands, "Why don't you do that?"

Building a strong marriage happens brick by brick, day by day. "Think about it," wrote Zig. "People who are successful at whatever they do reach their objectives by a series of little things they do each day. If you can work on the little things in marriage—remembering to say 'I love you,' calling during coffee breaks and bringing her flowers— you will discover a big difference in your relationship with your mate."

Chris said he learned another thing from *Courtship After Marriage:* When he travels on the road, he never puts himself in a compromising position. That means not going out to a nightclub and knocking down a few drinks "with the guys" when the day is done.

"Instead, I call Joy at 9 P.M. and talk with her and my boys, Christopher and Vincent, telling them how much I love them and miss them," he said. "Joy is my best friend, and she's beautiful to me. It's wonderful to feel this way. You know, I recently saw Zig with his wife, the Redhead, and they were holding hands. I mean, he's seventy-one years old! Man, I would like to be holding hands with my wife when I'm seventy-one."

Learning to Prime the Pump

Before my life turned upside down, I lived in the comfort zone. I was where I wanted to be: early thirties, happily married, three kids, and on the cusp of a promising sales career.

My position was performing inside sales for an insurance company—the dirty work. I made the cold calls and turned over any promising leads to the salespeople, who would go out and sell property and liability insurance to various businesses. There was no commission involved, just straight salary.

Yes, this was the bottom rung, but I had not pursued any schooling after high school. What I had going for me was my love for people, and I saw sales as something that I could be successful in.

My life was cruising along when I received a distressing phone call from my mother: Her husband, my stepfather, had been arrested on charges of sexually molesting my thirteen-year-old sister, Mandy.

Mandy had told a junior high classmate that her stepfather had been molesting her for years. Mandy's friend, alarmed by the news, immediately informed a school counselor, which prompted a police and Social Services investigation.

The next morning—a Friday the thirteenth—my step-father was released on bail, and when Mandy came home from school that day, things really got spooky.

Mandy discovered that our mother and stepfather were missing and that they had written several suicide notes. All the guns from the apartment were also missing, and I knew my stepfather knew how to use them since he was a deputy for the sheriff's department in Adams County, outside of Denver.

A search of the apartment netted nothing. My stepfather and mother had disappeared.

Social Services gave me temporary custody of Mandy. A few days later, my mother called, asking to speak with Mandy. She sounded like a totally different person, definitely not the mother I had known for thirty years. I could tell that she was mentally somewhere else.

I begged her not to commit suicide, that we could work things out, but she wasn't interested in listening. Depression had grabbed her by the throat.

Mom called several more times, but we could never make any headway with her. We waited in agony for four days before we received the dreaded news from the police department. My parents had followed through on their suicide threats, and now the news of their deaths was all over town.

We were told by the police that it would be a good idea to go to their empty apartment and remove all the valuables and keepsakes before somebody could break in. It was a bizarre experience for us to go through our parents' belongings before we had even buried them.

Meanwhile, Mandy was taking this very hard, as one

would expect for a thirteen-year-old. The Victim's Advocate Office put me in touch with a therapist who specialized in sexual abuse and suicide. My immediate family needed counseling as well—for the suicides, and for the adjustments that would surely come as Mandy became part of our family. Mandy was just eighteen months older than my eldest daughter, Kristen who was going through puberty and experiencing the typical confusion of adolescence.

Suddenly I was the mother of four emotionally needy children. I felt some resentment when I had to become a mother to Mandy, and I'm certain the resentment was mutual, but someone had to step in and protect this child, deal with probate court, and keep the family on an emotional even keel, even though there were times I had to escape to my bedroom and pour my heart out to God and tell Him, "I can't deal with this anymore."

Fortunately, aunts and uncles in the area provided family support. I needed their help because I was a crying mess in those days. They stepped in and made sure I ate and got some sleep.

I joined a suicide support group, which helped me through those "What did I do wrong?" questions, but it took eighteen long months before I calmed down and felt life was getting back to some semblance of normalcy.

Meanwhile, Mandy wasn't doing too well. Her after-school routine was to retreat to her bedroom and lock the door. She wouldn't eat dinner with the family; instead, she would take her meal back to her room. I had to practically break down the door to check on her. One time, I found her curled up in her dark closet, staring off as if she were somewhere else. When I called a psychiatrist and described her laconic condition, he told me that she was suffering from disassociation—an attempt to disassociate herself from her body to get away from all the pain.

Apparently, the pain became unbearable, and one afternoon Mandy attempted suicide. She overdosed on pills and we had to force feed her charcoal-like substance to induce vomiting. Doctors admitted her to a mental hospital, where she was diagnosed with post-traumatic stress disorder. A psychologist prescribed Prozac, which helped take the edge off what she was feeling.

I had to get to know Mandy. We were never really close because she is almost twenty years younger than I am. On top of that, we are also emotional opposites. I am an extrovert—a real people person—and I was raising my children to be outgoing. I believed that whatever was bothering you needed to let come out. *Don't keep it bottled up, where it can cause more harm,* I told the kids. My sister, however, had been taught to keep everything inside, and that was not good.

TURNING A BIG CORNER

As I was experiencing much difficulty on the home front, I was not functioning well at work. All my colleagues knew what had happened, and while they tried their best to help, it was too hard to be reminded daily that this is where I was when the double suicide occurred.

I switched to another sales job, this time in the telecommunications industry, and not long after I arrived, my manager announced that the company would pay for employees to attend a Peter Lowe Success Seminar in Denver's 17,000-seat McNichols Arena. The first speaker of the long day was Zig Ziglar, and even though he was scheduled to come on at 8 A.M., I wanted to be there. I had heard of

Zig Ziglar because I had grown up in Texas, where *everyone* knew who he was.

Even though the full-page newspaper advertisements had stressed how the Peter Lowe seminar could "ignite your sales career," I was hoping for something more. Yes, I had been relying on my faith in Christ in the nearly two years since my mother and stepfather's suicides, but there had been an awful lot of garbage in my life. I was slipping into severe depression, and the pressure to remain an anchor—to be strong for everyone else—was taking its toll. I had to face the fact that I had been raised in a dysfunctional family. I wanted to break the chain in my family and keep my kids from experiencing all of that.

I tell you, it took everything in my power to keep my family together. My youngest, Jonathon, was three at the time of the suicides, and he was probably a little too young to have it profoundly affect him, but not so for my middle daughter, Amber, or for Kristen. My husband, Michael, was having difficulty adjusting to the new family situation as well.

Amber was seven at the time, and the suicide wounded her so badly that she just quit trying at school. We had to get her into a learning disability program because she had stopped reading, comprehending, and writing.

But then Kristen told a friend at school that she was planning her suicide! Thank God the friend informed a school counselor about the conversation, and we were able to intervene and get her some help before she was able to make good on her threat.

This was the context of my life as I walked into cavernous McNichols Arena for the Peter Lowe seminar. First out of the box was Zig Ziglar, who strode onto the stage to thunderous cheers. He began talking a thousand miles a minute, but I heard every word. Then he walked over to a stand with an old-fashioned, chrome-plated water pump, and in that famous baritone of his, told this story from his childhood years of growing up in Mississippi:

At our home, we had a water pump adjoining our house on the back porch. When I was too small to reach up and use the pump, I watched my mother and older brothers and sisters pump water from the well for us to drink and cook with, as well as use for bathing.

Many years later when I was in the cookware business, I met two fascinating young men named Bernard Haygood and Jimmy Glenn. One day in a sales meeting, Bernard told a story of priming a water pump, going through all the motions and the gestures. It seems that Bernard and Jimmy were riding in the South Alabama foothills one hot August day and they got thirsty, so Bernard pulled up behind an old farmhouse and, sure enough, there was a pump on the well. He grabbed the handle and started pumpin' away, but it wasn't long before he realized he was not going to get any results by just pumping, so he asked Jimmy to fetch some water from a nearby stream.

Jimmy grabbed a pail and returned with some water. Then he poured a little water in the top of the pump to "prime" it and get the flow of water started. For you city folks, this is what is known as "priming the pump." Anyway, Bernard kept pumpin' away, but still nothing was happening. He quickly grew discouraged. "Jimmy, I don't believe there's any water down there," said Bernard.

"Yes, there's water down there," said Jimmy. "It just takes a lot of pumpin'." What Jimmy said makes several excellent points. First of all, you've got to put something

into life before you can expect to get anything out of it. That's true in education, business, marriage, sales and the church—anything you can think of. Second, sometimes it seems you do a lot of work but see no results, but you have to remain persistent by pumping and pumping and pumping. My friend Jimmy went on to say that the best wells are those with the coolest, cleanest, sweetest, purest and best-tasting water, and they are always deep. That makes an excellent point, doesn't it? As a general rule, things that have real value are things that require a lot of effort.

Anyway, back to the story. Bernard continued to pump. A question came to his mind: Just how much pumping am I willing to do to get a drink of water? *So in fatigue, anger and disgust, Bernard threw up his hands and said, "Jimmy, there just isn't any water in there!"*

Jimmy quickly grabbed the pump handle himself and said, "Bernard! We can't stop now. If we do, the water goes all the way back down!"

Boy, isn't that a great illustration about life? We'll never know how many students fail to get a scholarship because they didn't study ten more minutes per day. We'll never know how many promotions were missed because we didn't devote the same energy, excitement and enthusiasm to the job for just a few more weeks or months. We'll never know how many sales were lost because we didn't give the prospect another chance to buy. There are many lessons from the pump, but this I do know: If you will pump long enough and hard enough, the rewards that follow will be beyond your wildest dreams.

I speak from experience. My dream to be a speaker was born in 1952. It was 1968 before I was able to speak full-time. It took four more years before my career literally exploded in 1972, and it's been magnificent ever since. My message is clear: Keep pumpin'. Keep persisting. And when the water starts to flow, it will be a magnificent experience for you.

Hearing this story was perfect for me. I could totally relate to the need to keep pumping. If you stop pumping in the middle of priming the pump, no water is going to come, and you will have to start all over. It was like a light bulb went off inside of me. Hello! Duh! Zig finally put all the pieces together for me. What he said about the pump made total sense. I couldn't give up. I could be right there in life and not know it. I had to keep going.

During the break, instead of skipping out and taking off as I had planned to do, I wandered over to the sales table and purchased a three-set series of Ziglar tapes—*The Goals Program, Changing the Picture,* and *Developing the Qualities of Success*—along with a copy of *Over the Top.* Included in the packet was a little "affirmation" card—a four-by-six-notecard that said, in part, "I am an honorable person who is truly grateful for the opportunity life has given me. These are the qualities of the winner I was born to be, and I fully intend to develop these marvelous qualities with which I have been entrusted. My convictions are strong, and I have a healthy self-image, a passion for what is right, and a solid hope for the future."

An instructional card promised changes in my life if for thirty days I would read the affirmation card in front of the bathroom mirror first thing in the morning. I was also to read it just before I went to bed.

I had been slowly sinking and didn't know it. I needed

a change in attitude, not a change in latitude. When I went home, I read that affirmation card in the bathroom once in the morning and once at night, and my husband, Michael, thought I was nuts. I got to the point where I would shut the bathroom door and lock it so he couldn't disturb me.

Instead of letting the evening waste away in front of the TV, I read *See You at the Top*. As I sat on the couch reading, I thought, *Wow! This is great!* There was everything I needed to work on my attitude and my depression. And when Michael started seeing changes in me, his attitude changed as well, so I got the whole family involved. For Amber, who had been having learning problems in school, I made my own little affirmation card for her and read it into a tape recorder for her to listen to.

"Oh, Mom, this is so stupid," she said, but after a week or two, she got into it. We had needed a way to get positive thoughts into her subconscious.

When Kristen, saw that I was no longer my depressed self and was starting to smile, she experienced a complete turn-around as well. Our communication, which had been shut down, opened up tremendously. "Mom, I've got this problem . . ." she began saying to me.

Kristen and I have started a suicide support group for Colorado teenagers. We participated in the making of the Colorado Survivors of Suicide Quilt, and traveled to Washington, D.C., to present the quilt to lawmakers on Capitol Hill. We really want to help teenagers dealing with suicide.

And what about Mandy? With all the things she was dealing with—the suicides, the sexual abuse, being a teenager, having to start a new school—I didn't want to push her too hard. I tried to be there for her and let her know I was available at any time. Then I heard Zig say in one of his tapes that everyone needs a hug—every day! I listened when Zig said he gives the Redhead ten hugs a day, whether she needs them or not, so I tried that philosophy on my sister. You know what? Mandy responded to that natural affection, and we grew closer.

WHERE WOULD WE BE TODAY?

Five years have passed since my mother and stepfather committed suicide. I shudder to think where our family would be without Zig Ziglar. Not only did he remind me that I needed to keep priming the pump of life, but he encouraged me to believe that tomorrow is going to get better.

Zig has been right on the mark. Reading affirmation cards, thinking positively, setting goals, giving hugs, seeing the glass half full and not half empty—these Ziglarisms have changed me and those closest to me.

The greatest gift I received from Zig was the realization that I could have anything I want in life as long as I approach it in the right manner and do not give up. Five years ago I had given up, but then Zig came along to give me the desire to change.

Joe Schoenig

With a Leg to Stand On

After growing up in Clovis, New Mexico, I dropped out of college to get married and sell life insurance with the Washington National Life Insurance Company. As part of my training, I was introduced to Zig Ziglar and other motivational materials, which were a big help. After two years with Washington National, I decided to seek out a multi-line insurance company that offered many insurance products, including life, auto, homeowners, commercial, and so on.

One company, Farmers Insurance Group, in Lubbock, Texas, had an entry-level program to train new agents and put them on a guaranteed subsidy for two years. Farmers, however, insisted upon some minimum standards for its new agents: college degree, married, homeowner, some money in savings, and absolutely no prior insurance experience. My resume was a tad different: I had flunked out of college, gotten divorced, was broke, did not own my home, and was an ex-life insurance agent. I had everything they didn't want; I didn't have anything they did want.

It took me about five months to beg Farmers Insurance

Group into giving me a contract, but on a commission basis only. My first commission check was for $37, not much money, even in the early 1970s.

It was the mid-1970s and Zig Ziglar was starting to take off. I remember getting hooked by his top-flight motivational message. I was wearing out the Ziglar tapes and going to his seminars in Lubbock—the ones that Juanell Teague put together. The way I figured it, I had one chance in life to be successful, and this was it. With Zig's coaching, I began to learn more about setting goals and making long-range commitments to help overcome the day-to-day frustrations of the insurance business.

Eventually my insurance career did catch fire, and I've been with Farmers Insurance Group ever since and have been fortunate enough to make the "Toppers Club" twenty-eight times in a row. In addition, Farmers picks between forty to sixty agents each year out of the 15,000 across the United States to spend a week at a "Presidents Council"—an all-expenses-paid trip to discuss Farmers' future with the top executives of the company, and I've been chosen fourteen times. For that I say, "Thank you, Zig!"

THE UNEXPECTED HAPPENS

While I credit Zig for much of my insurance success, his principles really helped me during an intense family tragedy.

On August 7, 1991, we were on our way back home from a horse competition near Austin, Texas. We were traveling in the family motor home, pulling a horse trailer. About three miles from Abilene, an eighteen-wheeler suddenly pulled out in front of us. We smashed into the tractor-trailer broadside. The entire family was in the motor home: myself, Carol, and our two children, Coby, sixteen years old, and Amy, six years old.

It was amazing that we even survived the crash. The motorhome became a deadly trap—a twisted piece of metal. The "Jaws of Life" could not free us from the wreckage; firefighters and paramedics used air chisels and a winch truck to save our lives. We were trapped in the motor home for more than two hours.

We were rushed to a hospital, where doctors operated on Carol for about four hours, while I lay in the emergency room area, awaiting my turn. On the third night in the hospital, the doctor came into my room and asked everyone to leave.

"I thought you'd like an update about your family and yourself," he began. "Amy is just bruised and has some minor cuts and scrapes. Coby broke his neck and is in traction. In about three days, a neurosurgeon will take him to surgery. If we get his neck fused without it moving, he should be fine. If not, he will be paralyzed from his neck down."

My face turned pale, and a long silence filled the room. We both knew what I was thinking. "How is Carol?" I asked. "Is she still alive?"

"Yes, she is," he replied. "Her legs are broken in forty-five to fifty pieces, however. It's our feeling that because of the severe breaks and lack of blood flow, both legs will have to be amputated at her hips.

"As for you, your pelvis is shattered, and your femur has broken off the ball in your hip. We put a prosthesis in, and if there is enough bone in there to hold your prosthesis in place, your right leg will be about two inches shorter than your left leg. If there's not enough bone left, we will have to take your leg off.''

The doctor turned on his heels and left the room. I laid in the bed and cried and cried. *Lord, why me? Can you tell me why?*

It was time to pray, and as I prayed to Almighty God to heal our family, I started setting goals, just as Zig had taught me to do in my insurance business. First, I needed short-term goals: staying alive, rehabilitation, avoiding amputation of the right leg. I needed to get stronger so I could help Carol and Coby rehabilitate. Long-term goals would be having everyone home under the same roof.

That day in the hospital, I looked for things to be thankful for. I was thankful my family was still alive. I was thankful that I knew how to set goals and try to attain them. I was thankful that I had memorized Scripture so I could recall God's Word in my mind when I needed it most.

Over the next year and a half, God worked many mighty miracles. Coby fully recovered, except for a slight lack of motion in his neck. Carol endured surgery after surgery and began a long physical therapy program, but she kept her legs. As for me, the bone in the top of my femur and the top of my hip began to grind. I went to several doctors, but no doctor was willing to do surgery on me because I didn't have enough bone left.

At the doctor's office one afternoon, I said, "I've taken between 300 to 400 pain pills in the last sixty days. I can't live my life like this. Every time I walk or turn over in bed, my hip bones grind. Can't anything be done?''

More tests confirmed that the doctors were out of options. The news slipped me into deep depression.

I called another physician, Dr. Robert Salem, who was a client and a friend. He took an interest in my case and called the American Medical Association to see if he could find a doctor who would be willing to help me. Two doctors popped up: one in Philadelphia and another in my hometown of Lubbock. The local doc had been trained in England.

The new physician, Dr. James Burke, studied my records, and he believed he could surgically repair the leg. "We will have to stretch the right leg two inches for this operation to be successful. The very maximum your sciatic nerve should be stretched is one-and-a-half inches. If we stretch it too far, it's going to paralyze your right leg. You will either have to drag it the remainder of your life, or we will have to amputate. But if all goes well, we will proceed to put a new hip in.

"Those are the risks of your surgery," Dr. Burke said gravely. "Go home and think about that. If you decide you want to proceed, come back and talk to me."

I prayed about what I should do for a long time. I carried a legal pad with me constantly. Every time a question popped into my mind, I would write it down. I felt at peace about having the operation. Finally, I told Carol, "I'm ready to have the surgery."

On the morning of the surgery, they wheeled me into the cool operating bay. Just before he put me to sleep, Dr. Burke said, "Joe, I'm going to be standing at the end of your bed when you begin to wake up. I'm going to wave my finger back and forth. What I mean by that is that I want you to move your toe. If you can move your toe, I'm going to give you a thumbs-up sign. That means the surgery was successful. If you can't move your toe, then you are going to have to make the decision I talked with you about earlier.''

Amputation.

For the rest of my life I will never forget waking up and seeing Dr. Burke standing down there, covered from head to toe in hospital greens and wearing a mask. He moved his finger back and forth. I tried to move my toe. Not sure if I was successful, I held my breath until he jerked his thumb up and started crying. I started crying, too. What an unbelievable moment!

That's why I'm indebted to the skills of physicians like Dr. Burke and to the skills of great thinkers like Zig Ziglar, who encouraged me to seek and follow God's will and never settle for less.

Thanks, Zig, for teaching me: (1) to know the true meaning of priming the pump; (2) to see that the glass of water is half full and not half empty; (3) how to do a checkup from the neck up; and (4) to see that if I help enough others get what they want, I'll have what I want.

Thanks a zillion, Zig!

Alexander (Sandy) Berardi

No Longer Under the Curse

The family had a name for it: the "Berardi Curse"—a black cloud that caused misfortune to rain down on everyone connected with *il familia*. Dating back to the old country, the curse traveled through generations of Berardis. Even family members who boarded a ship in the late eighteenth century, bound for a new life in America, believed the curse followed them across the Atlantic. There was no escaping it, generations of family members grew up hearing. Something bad was bound to happen, usually sooner rather than later.

Alexander Berardi, called Sandy by friends, was raised in a middle-class neighborhood in River Edge, New Jersey. Because of the curse, the cup was always half-empty rather than half-full in the Berardi home. A defeatist air filled their three-bedroom house on Continental Avenue.

Sandy's father was a housepainter who worked long hours. He put food on the table but not much else, and while he wasn't a great businessman, he had his pride: *Il Papa* never dreamed of collecting unemployment when work dried up.

Mom worked as a nurse, which helped the family through the rough patches, and as a kid, Sandy never knew his parents had money problems. "I was the youngest child, born when Mom was almost forty years old," said Sandy. "She was worn down at that point, having to work as a nurse and keep the house going. I was an inquisitive child who was constantly into trouble, constantly experimenting, constantly taking things apart and constantly trying to figure out how everything worked. Consequently, Mom spent a lot of time with me, and by the time I entered kindergarten, I could read and write."

But his kindergarten teacher showed Sandy who was boss. When five-year-old Sandy proudly showed his teacher his newfound reading and writing skills, she put him in his place. "Don't you ever let me see you do that again," she scolded. "You're not supposed to be able to do that until you're in third grade. Don't you ever do that again."

That teacher's attitude may seem unbelievable, but the rebuke caused young Sandy to hate school. He had to learn at everybody else's pace, and if he pushed ahead, there were consequences. He discovered that life was easier when he played the role of class dummy. If he knew the answer, he didn't raise his hand. If called upon, he uttered the wrong answer. "I played that role so well that I began to believe I was dumb," said Sandy.

When the family moved and Sandy was hit by appendicitis in grammar school, he had to repeat a grade. Then he fell ill again and lost another grade. By the time he reached third grade, he was two years older than everyone in his class—and walking around with a figurative "dummy" label pasted to the back of his shirt.

In eighth grade, his teacher asked Sandy to stay after

school one day. "Why is it that you get A's in my class and are completely attentive, but everyone else thinks you're a problem?"

The teacher didn't accept Sandy's "I dunno" reply.

"We need to go deeper into this," said the teacher, who arranged a battery of tests.

When Sandy scored very high on his IQ test, the school made him retake it five times before they believed the off-the-chart results were for real. "Even though I went into that test a dummy and came out a genius, in my mind I was still a dummy and would never accomplish much of anything," said Sandy. "That was just the way our family was. We lived under the Berardi curse that everyone in my family kept talking about."

The curse struck close to home when Sandy's father became seriously ill and was diagnosed with stomach cancer when Sandy was thirteen. "My mother's mother and my father were dying at the same time," recalled Sandy. "My mother worked all night from 11 P.M. to 7 A.M. When her shift ended, she went over and took care of her mother, and then she came home to attend to my father. He needed someone to do his tube feedings, so my mother taught me how to do that, along with injections.

"Deep inside of me was a sensation that my life was about to go off in a very strange direction. It was the unspoken promise of a scared little boy saying to his father, 'The doctors may not be able to cure you, but I can.' From that point on, I spent most of my time in the local university libraries and medical school libraries, poring over oncology textbooks."

LIFE ON THE STREETS

Since he and the public education system never were on the same page, Sandy "graduated" at age sixteen when he quit high school. He took the GEDs and earned an equivalency diploma then entered college. "When Dad died, that was pretty much it for any hope of anybody paying for my college tuition," said Sandy. "So I left home and became self-supporting while I attempted to be a pre-med student at the State University of New York."

Medical research held Sandy's interest, as did becoming a neurosurgeon. Sandy managed to hold down two jobs, attend class and barely subsist. When he was twenty years old, however, and in his senior year, he ran out of money, so he took a short sabbatical from the books and began working three jobs.

Over the course of eight months, several disasters struck Sandy. His tiny apartment—the one he had worked overtime to furnish—was robbed. Nearly everything was taken, including his stereo, couches and other living room furniture.

A month later, Sandy lost his full-time job in a packaging plant that paid relatively well. His two part-time jobs, which paid minimum wage (less than $2 an hour in the mid-1970s) weren't enough to cover the rent.

Where could he live? Sandy packed what belongings he had left and began living out of his car. Since one of his part-time jobs was working as an orderly, he parked his car in the hospital parking lot and slept in it following his night shift.

But wait—Sandy's life got worse. His "beater" car was stolen, along with just about every worldly possession he had left. When he reported the theft to police, Sandy believed they would turn the city upside down to find his car, but no such thing happened. Several weeks later, however, police did find his car charred to a crisp in the South Bronx.

Sandy visited his old apartment superintendent and told him about his woes. "We had developed this friendship over the two years I lived in his building," said Sandy.

"Here, take this," the superintendent said, handing Sandy a single audiocassette. "Maybe you'll find something in there."

Sandy tucked the cassette into his coat and thanked his friend for the gesture.

Since he was homeless—and didn't carry an extra cassette deck in his back pocket—Sandy didn't listen to the Zig Ziglar tape for a while. He got work driving a cab and picked up odd jobs here and there, but when he wasn't working, he found his way into the local public libraries. They were warm and a free place to sit and relax for a spell before having to go back out onto the streets.

He found a cassette deck in one library and inserted the Ziglar tape. He liked what he heard, so much that he played and replayed the tape several times in a row. "That was a real turning point in my life because it was my first opportunity to hear somebody saying what I had never heard before," said Sandy. "Zig's messages was 'All things were possible.' I was worth something."

Still, Sandy knew he was in a big hole. He was twenty years old, living by his wits on the streets, working minimum-wage jobs. "Although it was the lowest point of my life, I did feel alive. Every day was a challenge. At the same point, I could have easily gone one way or another. Interestingly enough, I never turned to crime, never turned to drugs—that stuff costs money, and I needed to eat—and I never turned to booze."

His first goal was to keep working. After his car was stolen, he had to walk four miles to his taxi company through some tough streets. "I really didn't want to go to work," said Sandy, "but something told me not to give up, so I walked there. When I found out my job that day was to drive a business executive to Boston, I nearly turned it down. It was snowing in Boston. Long trips didn't pay as well in tips, and drivers work for tips. But I took the ticket anyway."

The client, it turned out, was a reluctant flyer, a pharmaceutical drug researcher. He sat in the front seat with Sandy and talked all the way up Interstate 95.

"Midway through the trip, he turned to me and said, 'Son, what's the matter?' " said Sandy. "I thought I had been hiding it pretty well. I could tell he was a kind man, a man who wanted to listen, so I just unloaded. He quietly listened for the next two hours while it all came out. The next thing I knew, we were pulling into his driveway, and he handed me two things: a fifty-dollar bill as a tip and a card from his wallet. I tried to refuse the tip, saying the company had already paid me, but he insisted and tucked it into my shirt."

Sandy also tucked the card away, and looked at it upon his return. There was a Scriptural quotation on it, from Philippians 4:13: "I can do all things through Christ who strengthens me." After reading it, Sandy decided to use part of the $50 to buy himself a small pocket Bible and the rest for food.

The spiritual food that Sandy received meant more to him in the long run. "I had heard Zig allude to some biblical principles on the tape. I found comfort and solace in the Bible at a time when I needed a lot of comfort and solace."

A PLACE TO LAY HIS HEAD

Sandy also needed a place to stay warm. He searched for a job where he could work indoors at night. For instance, his taxi company hired him as a dispatcher for its graveyard shift, giving him a low-stress job and a place to lay his head during the quiet early morning hours. His little office had a tape deck, and with not much to do, he must have played that Zig Ziglar tape ten thousand times, he says, "probably enough to mimic his Texas and Mississippi accents. I tried to find more tapes by the guy, but that was difficult in New York."

Sandy says he developed a close bond with the voice on the cassette. "Looking back, I could have been searching for a father-type figure, but there was a closeness there that is hard to describe."

As he sat in that dispatcher room each night, taking calls and listening to snatches of Zig Ziglar, Sandy kept his eyes open for the right people to suggest the right things to him—just as Zig counseled. Then he heard about an on-the-job surgical technician training program at the hospital where he worked as an orderly.

One of the job requirements was that if you were "on call" and lived more than fifteen minutes from the hospital, you had to stay at the hospital overnight.

That's easy, Sandy thought. As soon as he became a "scrub tech," Sandy volunteered to be on call *every* night. When told that he would have to stay at the hospital—where he was given a clean room, a warm bed and shower facilities, Sandy said, "Aw, shucks." Better yet, the cafeteria served hot meals for fifty cents.

On nights the hospital didn't need him, Sandy told coworkers he would be glad to volunteer in their place. Thanksgiving? Christmas? Hey, why not? Sandy became the most popular friend any scrub tech with family could have.

For three years, Sandy practically lived at the hospital while he saved money to return to school. Then Sandy learned that the U.S. government was offering full scholarships to students who would become specialists in epidemiology—the study of communicable diseases. Become a medical researcher for free—if he tested well.

That's all Sandy needed to hear. Four years later, he graduated at the age of twenty-three and took a well-paying job with an international health care company. But by 1981, he had come to believe there was a future for him running his own medical research company.

"Everyone I knew thought I had lost my mind when I told them I wanted to quit my job and start a company that performed investigative medicine work for insurance companies," said Sandy. "I had $600 and an idea, and I worked out of the living room of my rented home. I answered the phone all day and did my investigations at night. I took everything and anything that came in."

Family members began reminding him of the Berardi curse: "Are you out of your mind?" "Why did you spend all that time in school just to do this stupid stuff?" "Why don't you get a real job?"

It didn't help matters that Sandy was broke again. But as he drove from place to place, Zig Ziglar was Sandy's constant companion in his car. *You can do anything you want if you put your mind to achieving it. You can do it.*

Sandy Berardi did make it. By the time he turned thirty

years of age, his start-up company employed five hundred physicians, nurses and technicians. He had his first million dollars in the bank. After he got married, the company expanded, swallowing up several smaller medical companies. "I was just thinking about it this morning," said Sandy. "I've lost count of how many families have benefited from Zig Ziglar through me because of the thousands of jobs my companies have created."

Looking back at his life and seeing the various turning points he encountered, Sandy can't help but think of his late father and what life must have been like for him. Yes, he was a housepainter, but he was also an artist who had to drop out of art school in Chicago during the Depression and paint houses for the man who owned the mortgage on the family home.

"He was an artist trapped in a housepainter's body, and he was absolutely miserable his whole life," said Sandy. "Dad did nothing but project his misery and live his misery and die a horrible death.

"I thank God that people like Zig Ziglar were put in my path so that I was able to fulfill my dreams. To look back and realize where I have come from and what I have been able to do is a tremendous blessing."

Zig Ziglar

Up Close and Personal

A note from Juanell Teague:
Dear Readers: Now that we're near the end of the book, are you still wondering what makes Zig Ziglar tick? Are you still wondering what he is really like?

I've known Zig for more than twenty years, but it wasn't until I sat down to interview him for this chapter that I made some interesting discoveries. I got to meet Zig at a whole new level—a level of vulnerability that I had never known before. It's a level I want you, the reader, to get to experience as I did. What follows reveals an intimate side of Zig that few people know, plus a discussion of several turning points in his life.

Juanell: Zig, as you know, for this book we've been sharing stories of people who experienced a major turning point in their lives after hearing you speak live or on tape, or having read one of your books. Correct me if I'm wrong, but I know that you had a major turning point in your life back in 1972. Can you tell me about it?

Zig: Well, my first turning point was when I was ten days old.

Juanell: Ten days old?

Zig: You see, if it hadn't been for that one, the others wouldn't have taken place. The doctor had said to my parents, "He's dead," so they took me and laid me on the bed. My grandmother picked me up and started talking to me. And of course, she wasn't talking to me. She was talking to God, and He chose to breathe the breath of life back in me. So that was a major turning point for me.

The next was when my dad died. I was five years old, and we lived in the country near Yazoo City, Mississippi. Soon thereafter, we moved into town, where better employment opportunities for my mother were available.

In my first year of school, I contracted many of the childhood diseases—mumps, measles and whooping cough—and missed about four months of school. Mrs. Dement Warren, my teacher, came out to the house twice a week and spent about an hour with me, bringing me up to speed and giving me my assignments.

Had she not done that, I would have failed the first grade. Had I failed the first grade, I would have been drafted out of high school for World War II. I would never, in all probability, have gone to college.

Instead, I went to college and got into the Naval Air Corps . . . and this represented a third turning point because I never was interested in school. I was always working. I worked every afternoon after school —from the time I was in the fifth grade until I finished high school, so I really didn't have much time to study and wasn't much of a student when I did.

Juanell: How did you get into the Naval Air Corps?

Zig: When America entered World War II in 1941, I decided I wanted to try to get into the Naval Air Corps, so in 1943 I went to summer school at Hinds Junior

College to pick up extra credits in math and science. My buddies thought it was pretty ridiculous because of my grades. But I started the process in December of 1943, was accepted in January of 1944 and reported for active duty at Millsaps College in July of 1944. When I got in—and only five out of every hundred who tried made it—I felt a big boost of confidence. Maybe I was reasonably intelligent after all.

Juanell: What were you like as a child?

Zig: I was very small, weighing only 120 pounds fully dressed as a senior in high school. Things were tough financially for my family. I had an attitude problem. In those days, we called them "inferiority complexes." Now we call them "poor self-images." I used to fight everything that moved. If I got into an argument and couldn't settle it in ten seconds, I'd just bust 'em one. A Mexican boy broke me of that habit, incidentally, but I scared him half to death. He thought he'd killed me. But when I got into the Naval Air Corps, that was a confidence builder.

Juanell: Were you shy as a youngster?

Zig: A little shy. But not shy around the guys or in school. But one-on-one, I was.

Juanell: Would you say that your mother gave you a good set of values?

Zig: Oh, no question.

Juanell: On a scale of one to ten, ten being the highest, how would you rate the positive impact and negative impact of your mother?

Zig: She was as close to a ten as a human being could get. She had incredible faith. She constantly taught us little sentence sermonettes, which were filled with values like:

• "Tell the truth and tell it ever, costeth what it will. For he who hides the wrong he does, does the wrong thing still."
• "When a task is once begun, you leave it not until it's done."
• "Be a matter great or small, do it well or not at all."

Those sorts of things just saturated my being. When she was working, she would sing Bible hymns and spirituals.

Juanell: Was she a hard worker?

Zig: Oh, yes. Many times at night when I awoke to go to the bathroom, as I walked across the back porch I could see the light in the hallway. My mother would be sitting there quilting. Then the next morning, she would awaken us. Breakfast had already been cooked on a wood stove, which meant she was up early. She worked with her cows. She worked in the garden. She was an incredible example. And yet she always had time for us. Always nurtured us. There was never any question about her love for us. But there was also never any question that she wanted things done right. She was, from a character-building point of view, superb.

Fifteen, twenty years ago, we went to a family reunion in Yazoo City. It was a family pig-out. Average weight gain was three-and-eight-tenths pounds. We didn't eat until we got full; we ate until we got tired. We went to the grocery store to buy a smoked ham and a smoked turkey, and canned soft drinks. My wife, Jean—I call her the Redhead when I'm talking about her, and Sugar Baby O.K when I'm talking to her— got her checkbook and wrote a check. She automatically pulled out a couple of credit cards and a driver's license and said, "I'm sure you'll want to see these." The lady never looked down at the credit cards or the driver's license. She was looking at the name on the check.

"No. Around here, this name is all the identification we'll need," she said, and the clerk wasn't talking about me. She didn't have a clue as to who I was, but she knew who my mother was. My mother could go to the bank and sign her name to a substantial note with no means of income of any kind. Over the years, the bankers had come to know that if she signed her name to a note, the money was already on the way back. So that day I just renewed the pledge I'd made years earlier, that if I never left my children anything, one thing I would leave them was a good name.

Juanell: Let me ask you this question. You said your mother was close to a ten. Was there any part of her that was a negative?

Zig: Well, when I was a youngster, I didn't really appreciate the "switchings." There were about six steps to the back porch, and she could transcend all of them with one jump. She'd walk to the peach tree and a switch would fall out of it and into her hands. She didn't even have to reach up. It'd just fall out—at least that's the way it seemed.

I have to tell you, however, that I never got a whipping I didn't deserve. She certainly never used anything on me that bruised me or was in any way damaging to me. But it did hurt my feelings, and I have a low threshold of pain.

Juanell: What else impacted your life?

Zig: People are stunned when I tell them I haven't developed relationships with the presidents of many big companies because I generally work with the administrators in those companies. However, I have cultivated relationships with outstanding theologians, psychologists, psychiatrists and physicians. I can pick up the phone and call some of the most knowledgeable theologians in the country, plus some of the greatest psychiatrists, psychologists and physicians.

Juanell: Why have you been drawn to these types of folks?

Zig: Because we're physical, mental and spiritual beings, and when you touch all three bases, chances are pretty good that you're going to be all right. Now, that's the reason, Juanell, that I can speak with confidence because it's not what's coming from me, it's what's coming through me. Big difference.

I'm really a communicator. I'm a delivery boy. I'm a reporter. Before I speak, I spend from three to four hours getting ready for each speech, even if I've given it many, many times before.

Juanell: How do you spend those hours getting ready? What do you do?

Zig: I almost completely rewrite my notes. And then I'll put them down, and maybe after a walk or a shower, I'll get back to them. Then I start practicing—particularly the first ten minutes. I can almost give you verbatim what I'm going to say in the first ten minutes. However, it would be arrogant for me to think that just because I've done a talk a hundred times that I can stand up and do it again.

Juanell: You mean you don't memorize your speeches?

Zig: No, and a lot of people are astonished that I use notes.

Juanell: Where do you hide them?

Zig: I just put them next to the overhead projector, and as I walk behind the lectern, I make it a point to check my notes. Most people never know I've got them.

Juanell: What do you do to keep your speeches fresh?

Zig: There's always something—a new example, illustration, funny story—that I can work in as a result of investing this extra time. My creativity is enhanced as a result of this attention to detail. That's what makes the difference between a good talk and just another talk.

Also, because I read an average of three hours each day, I keep adding new material. This makes the old material far more usable because the new stuff acts as the catalyst and kicks up ideas.

Juanell: Can you give me an example?

Zig: A lot of people have heard me say that I lost thirty-seven pounds by losing one-and-nine-tenths ounces a day over ten months. The other day I said to a crowd, "You know, you're going to have to make some changes. I gotta tell you, some of them are going to have to be radical. But the good news is you can make radical changes one small step at a time.

"For example, hurricanes and earthquakes get all the publicity, but termites do more damage—and they take one bite at a time. If you'll learn one new word a day, in five years' time you can talk to just about anybody on just about anything. Research at Georgetown Medical School proves that when your vocabulary goes up, your IQ goes up 100 percent of the time—no exceptions.

"Now, let's tie that to something else. Millionaires, when you get right down to it, are boring. Example: Movie stars, TV stars, music stars and athletic stars make millions and millions of dollars and get all the publicity, but far less than 2 percent of all millionaires in America are in those four professions. Far less than 2 percent.

"Let me tell you about millionaires. They live in an average neighborhood when they could afford a much better one. They live in a small house when they could afford a much bigger house. They drive a car that's five or six years old, and it's not a luxury car. They prefer to spend their time at home with their families. They are probably married to the same person all these years. It's boring.

"However, they are happy, healthy, prosperous, and secure, and they have friends, peace of mind, good family relationships and a wonderful hope for the future.

"For example, did you know, according to an ABC News study, that people who win a multimillion-dollar lottery are more likely to be miserable one year later than a person who was in an accident and became a paraplegic? The lottery winner thought the money was going to solve all of his problems and he would live happily ever after—and, of course, it doesn't happen. With the paraplegic, every slight step forward gives him hope that life is going to get better.

"But it's always small steps, and what small steps do is generate hope. When I say lose one-and-nine-tenths ounces a day, everybody who's got a weight problem says. 'I can do that.' The reality is that you build a beautiful marriage, not by a glorious honeymoon and a big party at Christmas or New Year's but by the little things you do every single day with your mate. You raise positive kids by doing the little things every single day. You build a great career the same way. You become an honor roll student by the discipline you impose upon yourself every day.''

Juanell: Zig, have people in the last few years started calling you a philosopher instead of a motivational speaker?

Zig: Not to any large degree. People think of a philosopher as being some old fella, and they view me as a young one, even though I'm seventy-one. But as I tell audiences today, "You know, God hasn't promised me five more minutes, but I honestly believe I am at least ten, maybe fifteen years away from hitting my peak."

My career's in front of me, not behind me. I really believe that. A few months ago I was at the Cooper Clinic, and I stayed on the treadmill nearly three minutes longer than when I was forty-five years old and miserably out of shape.

Today, my resting heart rate is fifty-one. My cholesterol level is 156. My blood pressure is 122/69. While God hasn't promised me anything, I really believe God's got some plans for me. When people ask me about retirement, I reply, "Well, retirement's never mentioned in the Bible."

Juanell:I know for a fact that you are the most respected speaker this world's ever known. Do you realize this, Zig?

Zig: Careful, Juanell.

Juanell: No, you are! And it's the degree of personal integrity that you have.

Zig: Well . . .

Juanell: No, really.

Zig: You know, there's another thing I should tell you about my speech preparation. There's much praying before I give a speech, because I know I need help, and I believe in arithmetic. I believe that me plus God equals enough, so when somebody says nice things about me, I'm grateful for that. But I have a pretty fair memory, and I remember where I was and the fact that very few people were saying anything about me before God turned my life around.

Juanell: Can you tell me about it?

Zig: The story starts when I was in my twenties and just getting into my sales career. For two-and-a-half years, I struggled for survival, and we lived on a financial roller coaster—lights turned off, telephone disconnected, car turned in, etc. Then, at a company training session, Mr. P. C. Merrell, a supervisor, turned me on big-time, and for the next three years I went like a house afire. The first year I finished number two out of more than seven thousand salesmen. The next year I was the highest-paid field manager in the United States. One year later, I was the youngest divisional supervisor in the company's sixty-six-year history and set some training records that stood for years.

Two years later, I wrote the Dale Carnegie people and told them of my records and wonderful accomplishments. They kept the letter for a long time as a classic example of the worst way possible to write a letter; "I, I, I, I" had the most exaggerated case of "I" trouble I think anybody's ever had.

However, I went to work with a Dale Carnegie franchise on Long Island, and my family and I moved to New York in 1955. They hired me to help introduce the new Dale Carnegie sales course. The problem was I would leave home early in the morning when the girls were asleep, and when I came home at night, they would already be in bed. It didn't take me but three months to realize I wasn't about to raise my little girls that way. So we went back to South Carolina.

Then, as I tell people, "I stopped growing and started swelling." Over the next five years, I was in everything that came down the pike, all the get-rich-quick schemes. I was the "wandering generality" personified. I'd go to work at this company and immediately come up with some brilliant ideas that I just knew they'd want to implement immediately. They might have been in business a hundred years, but I could easily tell they weren't going to last five more years. I mean, it was obvious. And when they would decline to take my brilliant suggestions, I'd say, "Well, I don't have to put up with this. I can go somewhere else." And so it was a miserable time for me and my family.

Juanell: Why was that? Weren't you still financially successful?

Zig: One day you've got some money, the next day you don't. The next day you do, the next day you don't. You're talking about a roller coaster. I tried about everything that came down the pike. Finally I was so broke and in debt, I realized that I had to do something.

Juanell: How old were you then?

Zig: Well, let's see. It was 1961, so that means I was thirty-five.

Juanell: Life's middle stages, the early thirties, thirty-four, thirty-five, are major turning points. You had to do something. What was it?

Zig: I got back in the cookware business, which I had said I would never consider doing. But from the first day, I felt like I was back home. I finished number five in the nation that year in 1961, and the next year, '62, I was the number one salesman in the country.

In those days, you had to send all the credit orders to Dallas. When I'd make a sale, I'd airmail special delivery the letter to Dallas and ask them to wire me the money. I was the best-known person at Western Union for about a year, where I'd pick up the wired money. I'd double park right on Main Street, run in and the lady would either shake her head "no" or nod "uh-huh."

I will never forget the night I had a fabulous dinner party. I sold $1,995 worth of cookware. Now, in 1962, that was a lot of cookware. All of it was cash except for one $200 sale. When I got home that night about eleven-thirty, the Redhead and I sat on the bed and counted the money. We'd put the $100 bills here and the $50 bills here and the $20 bills and the $10 bills and the $5 bills, and then we'd rearrange it and we'd count it again.

Juanell: Let me ask you a question. Would I have liked you back then?

Zig: You probably would have, up to a point, because I was personable and friendly. But you probably would have liked me more than you would have respected me.

During those years, I had some really good times as I started moving from selling into speaking, and a move to Dallas in 1968 was a real highlight. In 1970, I moved into speaking full-time, but a slow start and some financial setbacks left us broke and in debt. And that is how it was until a big event happened in 1972. I think one of the reasons God let me struggle so long was so that when I turned my life over to Him and every facet of my life—including finances—dramatically improved, I would recognize Him as the source.

Juanell: How do you handle all the letters and praise that come your way?

Zig: I know I can't handle it, and that's because God has made it clear to me that I'm not the one responsible for this, and I have never forgotten.

Other times when somebody compliments me, I just simply say, "Thank you." As a matter of fact, those that know me best will tell you that the surest way to turn me off is to overdo the compliments. I don't like people I see on a daily basis to do that. It just bugs me.

Juanell: But perhaps they mean well.

Zig: You know, the Bible says God's no respecter of persons. That's another one of the things about my mother that was so important. As a child in the Depression, I grew up in one of the most racist and bigoted states in the country, Mississippi. In my childhood, there was no such thing as a black lady. No, she was a black woman. There was no such thing as a black gentleman. No, he was a black man. And I saw some kids calling a sixty-five-year-old black man "boy."

That was the mind-set. That was the racial prejudice at that time. You certainly didn't say, "Yes, sir" and "No, sir" to them, unless you were a Ziglar. My mother always told us, "One of these days you will stand in front of a color-blind Lord. So now you will treat your black brothers and sisters with respect and with dignity."

That was wisdom. My mother may have only finished the fifth grade, but wisdom is the correct use of the truth in the knowledge you have. And what knowledge she had, she made good use of.

Juanell: I want to come back to a big event that happened in 1972. What was that all about?

Zig: It's when God got hold of me and my life.

Juanell: But hadn't you always been a Christian, someone who went to church every Sunday?

Zig: And I'd been baptized, too. I had been in church probably two thousand times from the time I was a child. We always went to church, because it was the thing to do. The crowd I ran with went to church, so we went to church.

An old expression sums up where I was: "Going to church doesn't make you a Christian any more than going into a garage makes you an automobile." There are many people today who labor under the illusion that they are Christians because they think that going to church, coming from a good family, doing good things, never hurting anybody and loving everybody makes them Christians. There's not a word of truth to that.

Back in 1972, the Redhead and I met a woman everyone called Sister Jessie, an elderly African-American lady. A friend said we just *had* to meet this remarkable woman, so we invited her and her friend Ann Anderson to come to our Dallas home over the Fourth of July weekend.

They spent Friday night and Saturday night in our home. Sister Jessie walked in talking about Christ, she walked out talking about Christ, and all the time she was there, she was talking about Christ. She loved the Lord.

She really got my attention when she said, "God has been waiting for you a long time." That hit me right between the eyes. The other thing she said was "You drink a little, don't you?"

"Yes, I do."

"With the mind that God gave you?"

Again, I felt like I had been hit in the head with a poleax.

When I saw what she had—a close relationship with Christ—I wanted the same thing.

I knew who Christ was, but I never had any kind of relationship with Him. However, as I learned of God's love and grace, I decided that since I had done very little with my life outside of some sales, family and management success, I needed resources that exceeded anything I personally had myself. The promise of Christ seemed to fit my every need. With considerable excitement, I committed my life to Him, and I've never looked back.

I believe God honored my mother when He permitted this African-American lady to bring me into the Kingdom.

After that event, it was almost as if God was saying, I've let you waste forty-five years. Now I've got some things I want you to do. So I'm going to reveal myself and what I can do so that there will never be any doubt in your mind that I am God. That's what happened, and my life took a total 180-degree turn—and it was all for the good.

At that time, I started doing a long series of six-hour seminars for Mary Kay Cosmetics, and in the process, my speaking philosophy evolved. Those Mary Kay seminars allowed me to do a fair amount of listening and watching to see what was effective.

Juanell: Do you realize that it is pretty unusual to make this major kind of change?

Zig: I sure do. The morning after I was saved, I walked into the kitchen, and I probably had, oh, 250 of those little bottles of booze that you get when you fly first class on the airlines. I never drank more than three or four times a month, with two major exceptions: I got drunk twice in my life, and both times I vowed that would never happen again.

But I brought those little bottles home. I loved champagne and somebody had given me a case of champagne. I also had several other bottles of booze. When I got up that Sunday morning, I went straight to the cabinets and I dumped every ounce of alcohol down the drain. I also said I would never take another drink.

Well, I broke that vow on November 26 of that year. The Redhead and I went out on our anniversary to the opening of a German restaurant owned by her hairdresser. He offered us some wine that evening. Don't misunderstand. You don't go to hell because you drink or smoke, you just smell like you've been there. I had decided not to drink anymore.

In Proverbs it says the prince does not drink wine, and I'm just one step above that since I'm a child of the King Himself. And this child of the King just doesn't drink booze. Every time you do, it kills some cells. Doctors can argue all they want to, but the facts are that alcohol—one drink a day—will not extend your life. It just won't. One person out of ten who starts with one drink a day will end up with a real alcohol problem—and a much shorter life span.

If you were to take one hundred teetotaling men and/or women and start them all on one drink a day, and another hundred who remained teetotalers, the hundred who drink will not live as long on average as the hundred who don't. But that's beside the point. I took the drink after I said I wouldn't. When I got home that night, my seven-year-old son asked, "Dad, did you drink anything tonight?"

Juanell: Your son Tom asked you that?

Zig: Tom asked me that. And I said, "Son, yes I did." And that seven-year-old boy looked right at me and said, "Dad, I can't begin to tell you how disappointed I am in you."

Juanell: What possessed him to ask you that question?

Zig: As I tell people, "I've got a smart boy, but he isn't that smart." That was the Holy Spirit. I looked at my boy and I said, "Son, I'll tell you what. If you'll forgive me this time, you'll never have to forgive me again." And since that day, I've not knowingly had an ounce of alcohol.

Once on a flight they served a drink that I thought was orange juice. I took one small sip and could tell there was something else in it. Ever since then I've asked, "Now, is this just orange juice?"

Not long after I was saved, we joined First Baptist Church in Dallas. A few weeks later, Richard Peacock, the minister to adults, prayed a powerful prayer that raised chill bumps on me. A young girl had just been kidnapped. He prayed that God would build a wall of fire around her and bring her back safely, unharmed and untouched. God heard that prayer, and she was returned unharmed.

I prayed immediately, "Lord, if you will just build a wall of fire around me so that I won't be tempted sexually, financially, morally or in any other way, so that I will not have to use my strength to fight the temptation, I'll use that strength to serve You."

And Juanell, by the grace of God, I've had zero temptation. Now that doesn't mean a thought has never gone through my mind. That's not what I'm saying, because I'm a man. But it does mean that I've never considered breaking my promise to God to maintain that sexual, financial and moral commitment. He did build that wall of fire around me.

I've been super careful ever since I made that promise. For example, I won't go for a cup of coffee or a meal with a woman. If a woman wants to talk to me in a hotel, we do it in the lobby—where everybody walks through. I have just been very careful.

A reporter once asked me if I ever took my secretary to lunch, and I replied no.

"You don't take your secretary to lunch?" he asked.

"Of course not," I said.

"Well, why not?"

"Well, first of all, she's a very bright lady; she wouldn't go with me." Then I said, "Second, if I took her out to lunch once, I might enjoy it and want to take her out again."

Even when I have my executive assistant, Laurie Magers, or any other woman in my office, the door is always open.

I have also prayed, Juanell, that God would give

me eyes only for the Redhead. That He would give me an ever-increasing passion just for her. I tell you, she's the most unique woman I've ever seen. I cherish every moment with her. I wouldn't, as I told the reporter, risk offending her for a thousand lunches with anyone, because she's the one that counts with me.

Juanell: Zig, I know you're worried that people reading this tribute book might get the impression that you're too good to be true, too perfect.

Zig: If they get that impression, I'm doing a lousy job of communicating. Many people have said some nice things about me, but the word "perfect" was noticeably absent from their comments. Like I said before, Juanell, God is no respecter of persons, and I understand why because I know I'm human, and I know I still have a sin nature.

I can give you an example from just four weeks ago. One Sunday after church, our Sunday school class—a big group of thirty people or so—went out to a nice restaurant. After we had been seated, it became clear that just one waiter was going to be serving us.

I went to the waiter and expressed my concern, since I knew it would take an inordinate amount of time to serve more than thirty people. Later, as he was bringing the water, I again expressed my concern and asked if another waitperson was going to help. He assured me he would have help. But when the other waiter didn't show up and he started taking orders, my irritation started to build, and I asked him point-blank, "Are you sure somebody's going to help you?"

"Absolutely," he answered confidently.

"Well, *where* is he?"

"Ah, he's busy over there," the waiter gestured, "but he's coming over right now."

He continued taking orders. After a few more minutes—we had now been there over forty-five minutes—I again asked for another waiter, and he responded, "No, we don't need him. It wouldn't speed things up anyhow."

That remark frosted me. "You have got to be kidding!" I told him. "One person can wait on thirty people as fast as two can? Man, that's ridiculous!"

I had made a scene—a public scene—in front of a lot of people. It was evident I had lost my patience. Well, the next day, Laurie, my executive assistant, received a phone call from a lady in my Sunday school class. "I was very disappointed in Mr. Ziglar," she told Laurie. "That's not the way he generally is. He owes everyone an apology."

She was right, and I knew I had to apologize. I stood up before that Sunday school class and said, "I have an apology to make regarding my behavior in the restaurant last weekend. Let me tell you where I made the mistake. I let a young waiter cause me to react badly, and let me tell you the damage that was done. Number 1: My witness to him was probably permanently destroyed. Number 2: The visitors who were in our class that day might never come back to this class. My witness to them was destroyed. Number 3: For those of you who are on the fence, my witness to you was also seriously damaged. I deeply regret it."

I learned a lesson that day, which was a good reminder that I need to be continually vigilant in the future. We all do. Nobody is perfect, but we can all achieve greatness.

See you at the top!

Wasn't that interview with Zig Ziglar remarkable?

What made that interview special—more than a friendly conversation or a routine exchange of information—was Zig's description of how he found his faith, his mission and his future in his mid-forties after many years of roller-coaster living. Sister Jessie's words—"God has been waiting on you a long time"—hit him with such force that he made an 180-degree turn in his life.

Zig's experience, and that of all the people in this book who experienced major life changes, was a turning point nudge.

You will experience your own share of turning point nudges in your lifetime. These opportunities are no more than one-to-three minutes long. If you fail to act, these promptings will diminish, and you will miss a life-changing opportunity. But if you act, you will receive untold blessings. I have seen turning point nudges work in my life, and I've seen them work dozens of times in the lives of those I have coached over the years.

As I wrote earlier, my first nudge occurred on January 19, 1977, when I was prompted to get up from the couch in the middle of a Texas dust storm and drive to a mall bookstore to seek out motivational books. I was at a breaking point. I wanted to be the best wife, mother and homemaker—and yet I wanted and needed more.

Five months later, a friend introduced me to Zig Ziglar. After reading *See You at the Top,* I was prompted to call his Dallas office and order six tickets to hear him speak.

Following Zig's speech, I was nudged to walk down that aisle and ask what it would take to get him to come to Lubbock, Texas, to speak at a motivational rally in my hometown.

The rest, as the old saying goes, is history, from my promoting speaker rallies to founding People Plus. But God had another big turning point nudge waiting for me, and the result is this book. Let me explain.

In April 1997, a young man named James Usher heard me speak in Atlanta. He approached me afterward and said he would give anything to share his story with Zig. He, too, had experienced a life-changing event because of Zig Ziglar. I told James to put his story on video, send it to me, and I would see what I could do. Once I popped the video in, James's story curled my toenails. I knew the video would mean a lot to Zig, so I wrote him a letter and told him that when he had an hour, he should watch it. "You *really* impacted this young man's life," I wrote.

A couple of weeks after I mailed the package, Zig was on the phone. "Miss Juanell," he said, "tell me about this young man whose video you sent."

Zig listened as I outlined James's story.

"When I'm in Atlanta, I would really like to meet him," he said.

"I'll tell him that," I replied.

As we hung up the phone, that's when the turning point nudge happened. For me, it was like the Holy Spirit speaking to my heart, saying, *Show him the fruits of his labor. Let their voices be heard and bring hope to the world.*

I knew it was a nudge because I had not been thinking along those lines. God just dropped it into my mind—from out of nowhere. That's how I knew the idea was from the Lord and not myself. But questions crept into my mind: *You mean show Zig and the world how his message has changed lives? Create a tribute for Zig Ziglar? Why me? Aren't there other people who could do a better job?*

Although I was asking God these questions, I knew that if I didn't respond to this turning point nudge immediately, it would diminish. I grabbed my tape recorder, put in a clean tape and poured out my heartfelt message. It would be a letter to Zig, stating "I would like to do a tribute in your honor." I told him I would find people like James Usher whose lives had been changed and put them into a book to share Zig's message of hope.

I dictated my letter. I handed the tape to my secretary to type and mail. The letter went out accidentally without me editing it. *Oh well,* I thought, *I did what I was supposed to do. It's not up to me, Lord. Edited or unedited, it's in Your hands.*

Two weeks later I received a letter from Zig reluctantly agreeing to my proposal. As long as I would produce a book showing how lives were changed and not just toss a bunch of bouquets at his feet, Zig said he would support the project.

The result is the book you're now holding. In addition, a new not-for-profit foundation, called Living to Change Lives, has been established to place Zig Ziglar's character-building principles in schools and organizations. This will be accomplished by following the mission statement, which says:

To honor Zig Ziglar and his message of hope, by taking his character-building principles to young people in America and around the globe, thereby empowering them to make this world a better place for themselves and others.

Let me leave you with these final thoughts on the turning point nudges:

- Have the courage to act immediately on your turning point nudges so they won't lose their impact on you and others around you.
- Have faith. You don't have to know exactly what is in front of you or all the details. You just have to know that it comes from the Lord.
- Move forward every day. You must be faithful and obedient.
- Have an unshakable belief. You will experience setbacks and disappointments, but if you know the Lord is leading, you will never have doubts.
- Trust the nudges.
- Be proactive, not reactive, so that the fear and risk are diluted.
- Use nudges to grow in confidence, knowing that you have given yourself permission to act. You want to be doubt-free.
- Don't look back.

So the next time a turning point nudges your heart, know that something exciting is about to happen in your life. You are being given something that you—and only you—can receive and share with others.

Your life *will* be different because of it.

Our Mission:
To honor Zig Ziglar and his message of hope, by taking his character-building principles to young people in America and around the globe, thereby empowering them to make this world a better place for themselves and others.

Thanks a Zillion

Living to Change Lives Foundation
c/o People Plus, Inc.
PO Box 742047
Dallas, TX 75374-2047
(voice) 972/ 231-2831
(fax) 972/ 231-9402
(e-mail) JTea1@aol.com
e-mail) ThankZig@flash.net

Juanell Teague
Founder &
Executive Director

Zig Ziglar
Honorary Board Member
& Advisor

Board of Directors:
Dennis Parker
Coach Rutledge
Kathy McInnis

Advisors:
Lou Holtz
Dave Hurley
Robert Lightner
Bernie Lofchick
Peter Lowe
Dr. Frank Minirth
Dennis Parker
Nido Qubein
Jim Rhode
Naomi Rhode
D.W. Rutledge
Mark Warren

Visit our Web site
ww.livingtochangelives.org
www.ZigZiglarTribute.org

What Is "Living to Change Lives"?

"Living to Change Lives" is a non-profit 501 (c) 3 corporation that develops and distributes programs teaching young people the importance of responsibility, attitude, self-esteem, goal setting, and leadership. These powerful, proven character-building programs provide youth with the tools needed to face today's challenges, reach their goals, lead productive lives and empower other youth to do the same.

If you are saddened and frustrated by the violence and crime impacting our young people, but feel helpless to change things for the better. Take heart. You can make a positive difference by supporting the Zig Ziglar Tribute and "Living to Change Lives."

The wave of recent school shootings and violence only underscores how important building character is today in our society. We are all baffled, and ask "How can young people be so violent?" Sadly, character building is sometimes overlooked by schools and too often not taught in homes. We have the greatest need in history for this type of program which will help bring essential values to young people in a variety of settings including:

- Schools
- Community Organizations
- Churches
- Rehabilitation Facilities.

Programs

Coaching to Change Lives
Written by Coach Dennis Parker and Coach D.W. Rutledge
Coaching to Change Lives is a character building curriculum, taught daily by coaches to athletes, that improves performance by empowering kids to be better people.

I Can Program
Written by Zig Ziglar Corporation
The "I Can" program was written to give students an introduction to principals on which they could build a positive attitude.

Kids Empowering Kids
Written by Susan Abar
(in development, available Fall 1999)
Kids Empowering Kids provides students and young leaders the platform skills and practice to present information in a multimedia format to any audience with confidence and competence.

Teaching to Change Lives
Written by Coach Dennis Parker and Coach D.W. Rutledge
(in development, available Fall 1999)
Spin-off of Coaching to Change Lives, designed for students not in athletics)

Results of these programs:
- Overall improvement in attitude, self-confidence, opinions and thought processes
- Changes kids lives for the better
- Empower kids and give them tools for life
- Helps kids develop good self-images, social skills and work ethics
- Good students with morally aligned extra-curricular activities, eventually make strong pillars of the community
- Self-motivated kids with direction

How can <u>you</u> help to honor Zig and keep kids safe?
Visit our Web site at:
www.livingtochangelives.org or
www.zigziglartribute.org